THE COSSART CHRONICLES
A FAMILY HISTORY NARRATIVE

By Robert Evan Wheatley
First Published December, 2008,
Revised for Paperback July, 2011

IT IS THROUGH SHEER CHANCE OF BIRTH I FIND MYSELF LIVING IN THE GREATEST NATION IN THE FREE WORLD IN THE MOST PROSPEROUS OF TIMES IN ALL OF HUMAN HISTORY. BUT THE FREEDOM AND PROSPERITY WE SOMETIMES TAKE FOR GRANTED TODAY DID NOT COME ABOUT BY MERE CHANCE. AS CITIZENS OF THESE UNITED STATES OF AMERICA, WE ARE BLESSED BENEFICIARIES OF THE STRUGGLES, TRIUMPHS COURAGE, SACRIFICE AND THE BLOOD OF THOSE WHO WENT BEFORE. THE STORY THAT FOLLOWS DESCRIBES ONE UNBROKEN THREAD IN THE FABRIC OF OUR NATIONAL HERITAGE. THIS IS MY ACCOUNT OF MY MOTHER'S PATERNAL COSSART ANCESTORS AND THE HISTORY THEY LIVED AND MADE, DATING FROM MEDIEVAL FRANCE TO 20TH CENTURY ILLINOIS.

"ANCESTORS"

In faded, grainy images spirits whisper to me across oceans of time. Worn by hardships of an existence unknown to me, their countenances tell of trials of a time long past, when life was often brutally hard and usually brief. These are my ancestors, at once foreign to me, yet so inextricably linked to my very soul...

Their eyes penetrate the fiber of my being. Their voices echo through the corridors of my mind and speak to me, "Yes, I know you" they say, "for you are a part of me." They call out to me; they haunt me and draw me to them and make me yearn to know these strangers to whom I owe my very existence.

The mighty Vincent Nova explodes in the brooding velvet void, shattering the darkness for a moment, and then it is gone... At once destroyer and creator of life, it too inevitably must fade and go the way of countless billions gone before. Even it you see, is subject and servant of nature's immutable laws; part of God's unfathomable endless cycle of creation and death.

And by these images before me now I am once again reminded of my own mortality; how frail and fleeting human life really is; that we are, after all, but dust in the vastness of the Universe, the span of our lives, insignificant in the context of the Cosmos, a nanosecond in the continuum of the Ages.

Someone once said, a man is never truly gone until forgotten. If there is but one thing I could ask of my children and theirs, it is simply this; remember me when I am gone. Remember the good and the bad, the beautiful and the ugly, the wisdom and the folly, the strength and the weakness, but remember me...remember them...remember your roots, for in you, our descendants, lies our hope of earthly immortality.

TABLE OF CONTENTS

Foreword

Dedication

Chapter One: A Badge of Enduring Honor	Page 1
Chapter Two: The Odyssey	Page 15
Chapter Three: The New World	Page 25
Chapter Four: Under British Rule	Page 39
Chapter Five: The Charlemagne Connection	Page 47
Chapter Six: Dutch Culture and the Revolution	Page 59
Chapter Seven: The Great Trek West	Page 71
Chapter Eight: The Dark and Bloody Ground	Page 81
Chapter Nine: The Year of Blood	Page 101
Chapter Ten: The Illinois Cosats	Page 119
Chapter Eleven: Twentieth Century Changes	Page 139
Appendices	Page 145
Source Bibliography	Page 165

FOREWORD – THIRTEEN GENERATIONS

After the passing of both my parents I felt a yearning, belatedly to be sure, to reconnect and learn more about my family, beyond those individuals I could remember in my own lifetime. Beginning at first as curiosity, it quickly escalated to passion. Since then, reconstruction of my family tree has come in fits and starts, and in researching some branches I have become well-acquainted with what is referred to by many genealogy enthusiasts as the proverbial "brick wall." However, in the case of my mother's paternal Cossart and Cosat line, I was amazed to find a wealth of information has already been recorded by genealogists and historians over hundreds of years.

In the process of discovering my roots I found myself rediscovering and becoming enthused about the history I had often found boring in school, when I had been forced to simply memorize dry data of dates, events, places and names. In researching my family tree I was astounded to find many of my ancestors had played pivotal roles in the making of the history I had sometimes found boring in my youth. They lived in the times, knew and "rubbed elbows" with such legendary historic figures as Peter Stuyvesant, Benjamin Franklin and Daniel Boone! My own ancestors were among the patriots, pioneers and founders of our nation I had learned about in school! Suddenly, that which had formerly been "dry" history became personalized and alive to me.

As remarkable as their lives and the times in which they lived them were, I am certain my ancestors did not see themselves as makers of history. They, like most of us today, simply struggled to get from one day to the next, and in the process of day-to-day survival, tried to make their lot better for themselves and their children. In discovering the part they played in history while simply living their lives, I have come to better understand and more fully appreciate my own place in the context of the ages.

The timeline narrative to follow is a distillation of information I have gathered over nearly a decade from numerous sources, including the published findings of other genealogical researchers, historic texts, official public documents and private family documents. Specific quotes are sourced [in brackets] within the text, referenced to a general source bibliography at the end. In this narrative I will not attempt to give a comprehensive description of the entire Cossart family tree. Indeed, one could devote a lifetime of research to such an undertaking. Instead, with but few exceptions, I will narrowly focus on my mother's direct paternal Cossart lineage, while giving the reader some historical context describing the often turbulent and dangerous times in which they lived.

Below are listed thirteen generations from my mother's paternal French and Dutch ancestors, the Cossarts, dating from Fifteenth Century France through her birth in Twentieth Century Danville, Illinois. Throughout this narrative, for the first mention of an individual in my direct lineage, and in cases where an individual may be confused with one of the same given name of another generation, the number of that person's generation as listed below will be shown in superscript parenthesis [()] after the name.

1.*Thomas Cossart, b. abt. 1464 in Normandy, France, d. 1541

2.*Jehan Cossart, b. abt. 1500, Rouen, Normandy, France, d. 1585

3.*Jacques Cossart, b. abt. 1538, Rouen, Normandy, France, d. 1608/09

4.Jacques Jacob Cossart, b. 1595 in Picardie, France, d. 1681

5.Jacques Cossart, b. May 29, 1639 in Leyden, Holland, d. 1685

6. David Cossart, b. June 18, 1671 in Bushwick (Brooklyn), New York, d. January 30, 1740

7. Francis Cossart I, b. 1713 in Bound Brook, Somerset County, New Jersey, d. 1795

8. Peter Cossart, b. August 30, 1746 in Raritan, Somerset County, New Jersey, d. July, 1781

9. Jacob Reverend Cossart, b. September 11, 1773 Conewago, York County, Pennsylvania, d. September 10, 1822

10. David Cosat, b. October 10, 1812 in Harrods Fort, Mercer County, Kentucky, d. February 26, 1886

11. John James Reverend Cosat, b. March 31, 1844 in Blount Twp., Vermilion County, Illinois, d. September 3, 1918

12. Francis Marion Cosat, b. February 19, 1889 in Blount Twp., Vermilion County, Illinois, d. July 24, 1949

13. Dorothy June Cosat, b June 7, 1921 in Danville, Vermilion County, Illinois, d. April 25, 2002

*Note: Generations 1 through 3 above are contested by some researchers.

~ DEDICATION ~

TO MY DEAR MOTHER

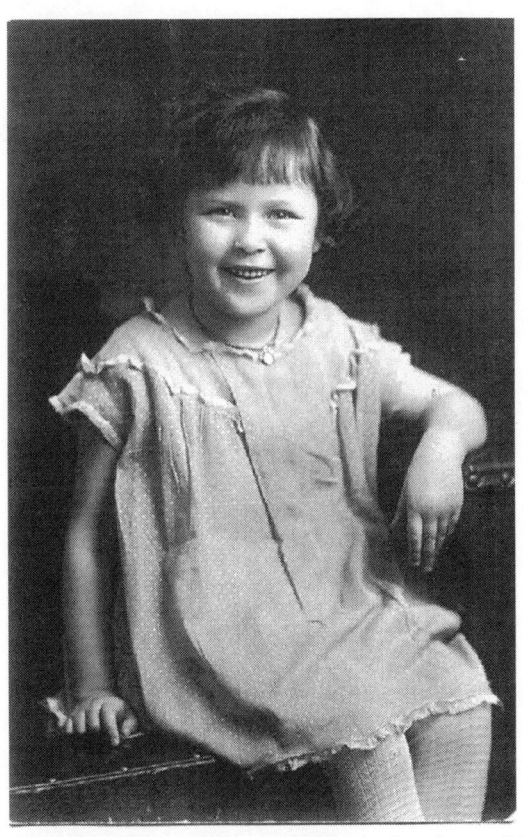

My mother, Dorothy June Cosat, firstborn daughter of Francis Marion Cosat, passed away in hospice care April 25, 2002. Sharing the Huguenot roots of the long line of Cossarts and Cosats before her, Dorothy had been a deeply religious person in this life with a strong belief in a new life hereafter. In the end, having lived a full life and being completely bedridden with no hope of recovery, she was at last ready, even looking forward to going to be with God and with loved ones who had gone before.

It seems appropriate it was in the spring of the year, as life on earth begins anew, her body was laid in its final resting place at Washington Park Memorial Cemetery on Indianapolis' East Side. I will forever cherish the precious memories I have of her, and I humbly dedicate to her as my labor of love, this narrative of her illustrious paternal family, the Cossarts. May God rest her soul and grant eternal peace and happiness to her spirit.

You gave to me the gift of life;
A gift that's not so small:
But I thank you most for the gift of your love:
The most precious gift of all

"Bobby"

CHAPTER ONE - A BADGE OF ENDURING HONOR

The Cossart family surname appears to have originated in Normandy in the north of France and can be traced back to the 12th century. It is said in the 14th Century, the family's social status leapfrogged from commoner to nobility when the family was awarded lands, titles and wealth in appreciation of loyal service to the king.

The exact place of origin of the American branch of the Cossarts is a matter of dispute among researchers. Some believe the American Cossart family descended from the Cossarts of La Rochelle, on the western coast of France. There it is said they held positions of high public trust, charged with protecting their harbor from foreign enemies. According to researcher Mary Ethel Tilley, "The tower of La Rochelle commanding the entrance to the harbor occurs in the Coat-of-Arms and in the crest of all the American descendants of the house of Jacques Cossart." [44]

On the other hand, in Huguenot Migration to America, 1885 [18], Charles Baird attributes the most likely place of origin of the American Cossarts, and others who came with them, to Normandy, Picardy and Bretagne. Joseph A Cossairt, Clerissa Tatterson and other published researchers concur with Baird, presenting compelling arguments the Cossarts of Liege (now in Belgium) indeed came from the Normandy and / or Picardie (Picardy) regions, later migrating to Leiden, Holland from Liege. Still other researchers dispute the connection of the American Cossarts of Leige to the Cossarts of Rouen in Normandy, arguing no records exist to document their migration to Liege.

The debate continues, and lacking hard evidence it may never be resolved. Whoever is correct, it can be stated with certainty the Patriarch of the American Cossarts, Jacques Cossart[5] of Leiden, Holland emigrated from Holland to the New World, departing with his wife and children from the port of Amsterdam on October 14, 1662. The descending generations from his father, Jacques Jacob Cossart[4] of Liege to my mother's generation has been solidly established by numerous researchers and is well-documented.

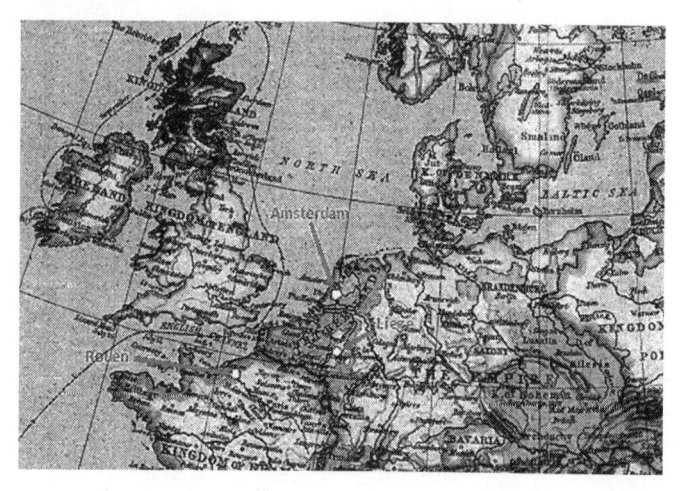

Jacques Jacob Cossart[4] was born 1595, most probably it appears in Picardie, France, son of Jacques Cossart[3] and Marguerite Toustain of Rouen. Rouen, the capital of Normandy lies on the River Seine between Paris and the port city of La Havre. Picardy lies to the East of Normandy and Southwest of Liege. Though undocumented, the presumed migration of the family appears to have been from Rouen, eastward to Picardie, thence northeast to Liege. As I shall explain, there were good reasons many leaving France in that age, including those of noble blood, did not wish to leave a paper trail.

The Cossarts were Huguenots, a group of Protestants of the Reformed Church, established 1550 by John Calvin. Jacques'[4] father would probably have been about 12 at the time of the Calvin Reformation, and he was brought up following the teachings of Calvin. The Calvinists were highly critical of the religious dogma of the Catholic Church. But in 16th Century France, those whose beliefs ran contrary those of the mighty Holy Roman Catholic Church were ostracized and persecuted from the beginning. Like the early Christians of the Roman Empire who faced persecution for their beliefs and death at the hands of the Pagan Romans, the faithful followers of Calvinism in the 16th Century out of necessity met only in secret in private places in the homes of like-minded believers.

Although the origin of the term Huguenot is uncertain, it is said by some to mean "sworn brother." Others say it derived from the Flemish words, "Huis genooten", meaning "House fellows"– those who meet in houses to pray, rather than in churches. There are other theories regarding the origin of the name, but it is generally agreed it was a derogatory term, used by the Catholic majority in referring to those of Protestant faith. Derogatory it may have been, but as O.I.A. Roche writes in The Days of the Upright, A History of the Huguenots, 1965 [49] "...the word became, during two and a half centuries of terror and triumph, a badge of enduring honor and courage."

La Croix Huguenote, a meld of the Maltese Cross and Fleur de Lys with pendant dove attached, was worn by the Huguenots as a silent means of recognition amongst themselves, the dove symbolizing the presence of the Holy Spirit through all life's adversity. As the Puritans and Separatists of England in that age sought refuge from persecution by the government sanctioned Church of England, so the Huguenots sought refuge from the literally murderous persecution of the Roman Catholic Church in France by fleeing to Holland, Germany and other countries in waves of emigration in the 1600's. The following is from the journal of Daniel Trabue [5], a Huguenot descendant, penned about 1820.

"...the Catholic Church as it existed in Western Europe in the seventeenth century had become so corrupt and secularized that it defied not only the teachings of Christ, but the commandments of God. Christ taught that salvation is free and is the gift of God, not something that can be bought by passing money to a priest to secure his indulgence. The Huguenots felt that such a practice was undoubtedly sinful in the eyes of God. And the worship of relics was certainly seen as a blatant violation of the second commandment forbidding idolatry. These courageous people, driven by their conscience, their faith, their zeal, and their vision of being able to worship in freedom, according to their newly found Reformed doctrine, felt that they had no alternative but to flee France and find a new home where they would have religious freedom."

Because of their open criticism of the practices of the politically powerful Roman Catholic Church, and probably more importantly, because of their refusal to tithe to the Catholic Church, many thousands of unarmed Huguenots were massacred in the 16th and 17th Centuries with active participation by the Catholic Clergy and full approval and encouragement of the Papacy. On Saint Bartholomew's Day, August 24, 1572, a diabolical plot, hatched by the Queen Mother, Catherine de Medici, and somewhat reluctantly acquiesced to by her son, King Charles IX, to cleanse the French population of the troublesome Huguenot heretics was set into motion. Paris, a staunchly pro-Catholic and violently anti-Huguenot city, witnessed the beginning of a wave of very public mass murders of Huguenots that would continue for months. Beginning as a plot to assassinate the leaders of the Huguenot movement, it swiftly turned into a general massacre of any and all who could be identified as Protestant. Because many Huguenots were merchants or of noble blood and were relatively well off economically, in many cases, simply living in a fine house was proof enough of being Huguenot. Led in a "Holy War" by French soldiers and Catholic Clergy, the common people soon joined in the slaughter. A seething, raging torrent of hatred and jealousy was unleashed, sanctified by the Church, and in an orgy of death, the gutters of Paris literally coursed red with Huguenot blood.

Streets were blocked with chains to prevent Protestant families escaping their neighborhoods. Going house to house, the mobs dragged entire families screaming from their homes into the street where men, women and children were butchered indiscriminately, simply because they were, or were suspected to be of Protestant faith. Huguenot possessions not immediately appropriated by the soldiers and clergy became booty for looters. Even the blood-soaked clothing of the slain was stripped from the lifeless corpses and given over to the Catholic poor. Last in line for the plunder, like jackals they waited their share, gleaning whatever scraps were left by the predators higher in the pecking order.

The torment and abuse of the victims continued even in death. Each day new legions of corpses were strung up to hang for days in the streets, faces frozen in masks of terror, vacant, staring eyes to be pecked out by the crows, their disemboweled carcasses spurned, reviled and spat upon by the public. For months the air of Paris hung thick and fetid with the smell of death. There were no funerals or wakes for the victims of this nightmare. Stripped of all human dignity, their defiled remains, unworthy of a decent Christian burial, were simply heaped upon carts and trundled away to the river for disposal like so much malodorous garbage. Not limited to Paris, the mob insanity spread to Toulouse, Bordeaux, Lyon, Bourges, Rouen, and Orléans. And all was justified, invoking the name of God, and claiming these "Holy" works were wrought with His blessing.

"Beginning at Paris, the French soldiers and the Roman Catholic clergy fell upon the unarmed people, and blood flowed like a river throughout the entire country. Men, women, and children fell in heaps before the mobs and the bloodthirsty troops. In one week, almost 100,000 Protestants perished. The rivers of France were so filled with corpses that for many months no fish were eaten. In the valley of the Loire, wolves came down from the hills to feed upon the decaying bodies of Frenchmen. The list of massacres was as endless as the list of the dead!" [62]

Jacques-Auguste de Thou was a young man at the time of the massacre. Decades later, recalling the horror he witnessed, he recorded his unforgettable memories for posterity. "...the streets and ways did resound with the noise of those that flocked to the slaughter and plunder, and the complaints and doleful out-cries of dying men, and those that were nigh to danger were every where heard. The carkasses of the slain were thrown down from the windows, the Courts & chambers of houses were full of dead men, their dead bodies rolled in dirt were dragged through the streets, bloud did flow in such abundance through the chanels of the streets, that full streams of bloud did run down into the river:

the number of the slain men, women, even those that were great with child, and children also, was innumerable." [2]

"...the Seine as it rolled through Paris seemed but a river of blood; and the corpses which it was bearing to the ocean were so numerous that the bridges had difficulty in giving them passage, and were in some danger of becoming choked and turning back the stream, and drowning Paris in the blood of its own shedding. Such was the gigantic horror on which the sun of that Sunday morning, the 24th of August, 1572 –St. Bartholomew's Day – looked down." [11]

Incredible as it sounds, it is recorded when news of the grisly slaughter reached the Vatican, cannons roared in celebration, and the bells of every church in Rome rang out in peals of jubilation. Pope Gregory XIII, ebullient at the news, joyfully ordered a commemorative gold medallion struck in honor of the occasion. The front bore the image of the Pope. On the obverse was the image of the Angel of God, clutching the righteous sword of Almighty vengeance, hovering over the bodies of the slain lying in the streets. The triumphant inscription in Latin proclaimed, "Slaughter of the Huguenots 1572."

Not satisfied with just a medallion, Gregory commissioned Italian artist Giorgio Vasari to paint frescos in the Vatican, depicting that for which the Pope gave thanks in prayer as "a glorious triumph over a perfidious race."[34] Though a hideously misguided and perverted church celebrated the unholy carnage with unabashed glee and satisfaction at the time, today, in a more enlightened age, the frescos remain; not in celebration, but as a stark and brutally honest reminder of a dark and shameful era in the history of the Roman Catholic Church. They stand an undeniable testament to the unspeakable evil too oft perpetrated by man in the name of God.

Certainly, this was not the first time in history in which innocent humanity was brutally butchered at behest of government-sanctioned radical religion, nor would it be the last. It was but one episode in a long series of bloody Crusades embarked upon by the Church. In contrast to the days of the gentle early Christian martyrs who lived humble lives, having taken vows of poverty, by the Sixteenth Century almost the entire Church hierarchy had become corrupted by power and imbued with an insatiable lust for wealth. One of the most highly revered of the early martyrs, Saint Paul in his Epistle to Timothy warned, "The love of money is the root of all evil."

The Church had apparently forgotten or conveniently ignored Paul's warning, for all evil perpetrated or sanctioned by the Medieval Catholic Church seemed to have at its root the love of money. Furthermore, the Church well understood wealth was accumulated through control of the masses. Those who would not be controlled, specifically the Huguenots, had to be destroyed. And all was justified, disguised as righteous Holy works and unflinchingly carried out with self-confident and pious religious zeal. "High ideals were besmirched by cruelty and greed, enterprise and endurance by a blind and narrow self-righteousness; and the Holy War itself was nothing more than a long act of intolerance in the name of God." [47]

Today, some will argue the persecution of the Huguenots was not rooted in religious intolerance at all, but was based solely upon the political threat they represented to the power establishment; the persecution and death they suffered was a natural result they had brought upon themselves for the civil unrest their leaders were fomenting. Such a position might seem to cast the Huguenots as simply a disruptive, rebellious minority in an otherwise peaceful, well-ordered society, perhaps even deserving of what they got. The fact they presented a political threat to the establishment is undeniable. But in that age, politics and religion were inextricably linked. The civil unrest was part and parcel of the Huguenot struggle for religious freedom. The political threat the Protestants posed the Catholic power structure was based entirely upon their dissenting religious beliefs and their rejection of the dogma and the authority, of the Catholic Church and her co-dependents in the French Monarchy.

Although a minority in France, which was highly regarded by the Vatican as a jewel in the Crown of Catholicism, the numbers of the Protestants were growing, and the less than endearing qualities of the Huguenot belief system earned for them the label, "heretic." It was by this device, this label heretic, the Sixth Commandment, "Thou shall not murder" was selectively applied, rendered non-applicable in the case of the Huguenots. Such being the case, any and all measures taken to eradicate them from France were justified in the minds of many Catholic faithful. Death and destruction of the Huguenots was regularly preached from Holy Catholic pulpits.

To maintain its grip on power, the Church required an unquestioning and obedient population. As always, it was primarily the educated and economically independent that dared disobey and question the practices of the establishment. The poor vast ignorant masses on the other hand, content with the scraps doled out by powers that be, rabidly opposed anything that might destabilize and threaten their status quo. To France's great national detriment, continuing religious persecution of the "heretic" Huguenots and other dissenting religious groups in the 16th and 17th Centuries was responsible for exodus of a significant portion of the population to other countries. And the majority of these were not the poor illiterate rabble of lower-class society, but were noblemen, well-educated middle-class businessmen, skilled tradesmen and artisans – the bulwark and strength of any civilized society. Over time, the French population would thereby become increasingly polarized in a two-caste system, made up of a vastly wealthy ruling class and the incredibly poor commoner.

France's loss was others' gain, however. James Riker in History of Harlem, 1881 [13], quotes French historian Charles Maurice Davies. "The fugitives were not criminals escaped from justice, speculators lured by the hope of plunder, nor idlers coming thither to enjoy the luxuries which their own country did not afford: they were generally men persecuted on account of their love of civil liberty, or their devotion to their religious tenets. Had they been content to sacrifice the one or the other to their present ease and interest, they had remained unmolested where they were; it was by their activity, integrity and resolution that they rendered themselves obnoxious to the tyrannical and bigoted governments which drove them from their native land; and these virtues they carried with them to their adopted country, peopling it, not with vagabonds or indolent voluptuaries, but with brave, intelligent and useful citizens."

Ultimately, persecution by government-sanctioned churches in France and elsewhere lent tremendous impetus to the colonization of the New World by pilgrims seeking religious freedom and opportunity for a better life. And there in that New World a new nation would eventually emerge – a nation whose Constitution would be rooted in tenets of tolerance and religious freedom for all, and stringently opposed to any form of government-mandated religion; a principle today commonly, but somewhat erroneously referred to as "separation of Church and

State."

Having survived the terrible bloodletting of the 1572 massacres, Jacques[3] and other Huguenots, were nonetheless destined to endure decades of persecution thereafter. In an effort to bring peace to a land torn by religious strife, the 1598 Edict of Nantes eventually granted Huguenots some limited legal rights to assemblage and worship. In essence, it acknowledged their right to exist and their right to believe as they did. This was in itself, a significant concession to the Huguenots by the Monarchy, and doubtless invoked the ire of many a Catholic, both among the lay people and the clergy. Even so, by no means did the edict grant equal treatment under law. Although the King's true sympathy lay with the Huguenots, Henry IV, who was raised a Protestant himself, fully comprehended the immense political power wielded by the Catholic Church. Next in line for succession after the death of Henry III, he had been allowed to ascend to the throne in 1594 only after publicly renouncing his Protestant faith, privately conceding, "Paris is worth a mass." [63]

In much of Medieval Europe, the reality was, the Catholic Church and the State formed a symbiotic dual power structure that shared control over the people. The Monarchy held the reins of Royal government, but to a large extent its power issued from and was modulated by the Roman Catholic Church. The Monarchy held power over life and death and the destiny of the common man in the temporal world. But to the great unwashed masses, the Catholic Church alone was vested with power over the destiny of their eternal souls, and her Holy priests possessed the keys to Heaven and Hell. Only through the Church could they hope to gain absolution for their sins and be admitted to Paradise. The eternal trumped the temporal.

In order to avoid complete alienation of the Church and the Catholic majority, King Henry IV pragmatically upheld many civil and religious restrictions on the Huguenots in his nonetheless historic edict. Assemblage and worship was to be restricted to specific approved cities or in places outside Catholic city walls. Huguenots were still expected to tithe to the Catholic Church, observe Catholic holidays and be bound by Catholic law governing marriage. They were not allowed to school their children in their homes. The only education allowed or recognized by the State was that administered by the Catholic Church. Though the Edict was later revoked, it did temporarily improve the lot of the Huguenots to some extent. However, no edict could erase with the stroke of a pen the deep-seated resentment and hatred for Huguenots among the Catholic majority, and periodic random murders of Protestants continued, regardless.

Lest the reader misunderstand the intent of the writer, the content of this chapter has been offered solely to frame and describe briefly the historic events that contributed to the sweeping changes taking place in the religious, social and political fabric in Europe, particularly in France, and the struggles and hardships that drove the Cossarts and others like them to abandon their ancestral homelands to seek a better life elsewhere. About 1607 Jacques[3] at last cut ties with the land of his nativity and removed with his family to the City of Liege where they could openly practice their religion and school their children in the way of their faith without fear of recrimination from the Catholic Church-State. Fleeing the endless religious wars and bloody civil turmoil of France, thus began a decades-long odyssey that would ultimately bring the Cossarts to new beginnings in a strange and wonderful New World beyond the sea.

A Huguenot on St. Bartholomew's Day - John Everett Millais

CHAPTER TWO - THE ODYSSEY

In the mid-16th Century, concurrent with the Huguenot persecution in France, a strong Protestant movement had also developed in the Netherlands. As disaffection with the ruling Catholic Spanish King, Philip II grew, general unrest and anti-Catholic riots spread across the region. In 1579, the Union of the Utrecht was formed of the Northern provinces and a few Southern provinces whose populations were largely Protestant. However, most Southern provinces and cities, including the city of Liege where the Cossarts eventually settled chose not to join in the Union, but later united to form the country of Belgium. Because of these developments, much of the Netherlands, particularly Holland, became a magnet, attracting Protestants from all over Western Europe.

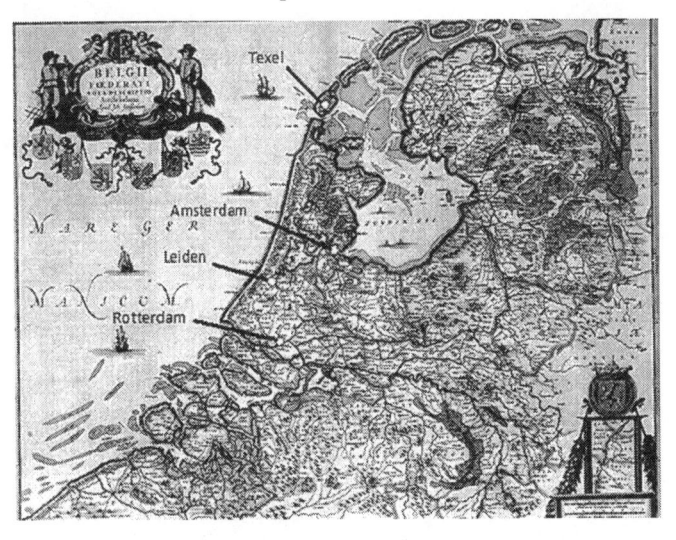

In 1630 Jacques'[3] son, Jacques[4], at age 35 married Rachael Gelton, born 1610 in Liege. Records indicate Jacques and Rachael migrated from Liege to Leiden, Holland shortly after their wedding. In Leiden, the last great city on the Rhine before it empties into the North Sea, their first child, Rachael, was born in 1632. My 7th Great Grandfather, Jacques Cossart[5] was born there seven years later in 1639. Dutch Reformed Church records document he was baptized May 29 that year.

While in Holland, a land of freedom and opportunity in its own right, the Cossart family ascended to considerable political importance and power. It is claimed Jacques Cossart[4] became Burgomeister (Mayor) of Rotterdam, and he was buried there with great civil honors. The family crest is said to be inscribed on his tomb. Some researchers do question whether this was the same Jacques Cossart, who was father of the patriarch of the American Cossarts, or perhaps a member of another branch of the family. The 1658 map of the Netherlands above shows the relative locations of Leiden and Rotterdam, which were not far-removed one from the other.

On August 14, 1656, Jacques Cossart[5] of Leiden wed Lea Villeman, a.k.a., Lydia Willems in the Walloon Church of Frankenthal, Bavaria, a village of Huguenot refugees. It is uncertain whether Lea was born in Leiden or in Frankenthal. Apparently moderately well-off financially, Jacques and Lea lived in a manor in Frankenthal for a time after their wedding. Their children born there include Lea Cossart I, baptized on May 31, 1657, Rachael, baptized November 11, 1658, and Susanna, baptized February 3, 1661. The couple must have traveled at least occasionally between Leiden and Frankenthal, as records show them received back into the church at Leiden in December, 1659. Church records also show they again returned to Frankenthal several months later on April 7, 1660.

In 1662 Jacques and Lea left Frankenthal for the last time, bound for the port city of Amsterdam. Apparently their second daughter, Rachael, had died by then, for they departed Amsterdam with only two daughters, one aged 5 years, the other 18 months, seeking greener pastures in the Dutch Colonies of

America aboard the ship "De Purmerlander Kerk." What a leap of faith it must have required to abandon the familiar surroundings of their native Europe to begin life anew in a strange land of promise and peril – one they had never before seen, except perhaps in their dreams!

"Such moral courage as they exhibited, especially the refugees, commands admiration; such trials as they endured when called to resist or flee oppression, appeal to our sympathies! Clinging to their faith or principles though at the cost of their peace and safety, and all the endearments of home, country and kindred; choosing rather to venture the treacherous ocean and the dangers of an untried wilderness where still was sovereign the savage and the beast of prey,—and all to secure the sacred boon of liberty denied them in their native lands; do they not deserve the first place in history, and in the grateful remembrance of those who are reaping the benefits of their labors and sacrifices?" [13]

Indeed, I have often tried to put myself in their place and gain an appreciation of what that eventful morn must have been like for them. It was a Saturday, October 14, 1662, when under command of Captain Benjamin Barents, the ship with supplies for the colony and passengers and crew numbering about ninety weighed anchor and set sail for the New World. As the morning wind freshened and billowed her canvas, the ship abandoned the safety of Amsterdam harbor and slipped into the open but shoal-filled waters of the inland waterway, known then as the Zuyder Zee.

A Dutchman by birth, Jacques' spiritual bonds and gratitude to mother Holland, which had welcomed and freely provided the Cossart family refuge from the religious persecution they had so long endured in France, surely must have run deep. Knowing they were forever leaving behind the friendly and familiar environs of the Netherlands, Jacques and Lea must have been awash with mixed emotions. Experiencing a sense of elation for the adventure that lay ahead, tempered by not inconsiderable melancholy at leaving the fair land of his birth, Jacques as head of his family almost certainly must also have felt some trepidation for the long and perilous voyage to which he had committed himself, his wife and their two young daughters. Having safely avoided the shoals of Zuyder Zee and negotiated the Straits of Texel, the Cossarts and their traveling companions might have lined the deck for one last lingering look and to bid final farewell to the last soil of the Netherlands most of them would ever lay eyes upon.

Mostly families bound for the colonies they hailed from Denmark, Holland, France and Germany. They were Claes Pulusz of Ditmarsen, Denmark with his wife, Nicholas DuPuis, his wife and three children from Artois, France, Ernou DuTois from Lisle, France with wife and child, Gideon Merlet, with wife and four children, Louis Lackman, wife and three children, Jan De Concilie, Jan Bocholte with wife and five children, Jacob Colff from Leiden with wife and two children, Judith Jansz, a maiden from Leiden, Carsten Jansen, Ferdinandus De Mulder, Isaac Verniele with his wife and four children, Abelis Setskoorn and Claes Jansen Van Heyningen. Regardless of their origins or their marital status, there was one hope uniting all – the hope of making a better life in a New World.

Now heading out into the deeper waters of the North Sea, the ship turned her bow southward. Within days Purmerlander Kerk, a square-sailed Dutch merchant vessel very much like the Mayflower in size and configuration, entered the Channel separating the French and English coastlines and made her way toward the gateway to the Atlantic. Skirting the southern coast of Great Britain, she passed in succession the cliffs of Dover, Portsmouth and Plymouth and finally, the tip of the southernmost peninsula of Great Britain, the jumping off point for trans-oceanic voyages, known to mariners as the "lizard head." Thereupon committing themselves to the crossing, ninety brave souls, doubtless borne on the wings of as many a fervent prayer, at last plunged headlong into the vast open Atlantic. Soon losing sight of all land, swallowed up in the limitless expanse of sea and sky the ship and humanity aboard her would shrink to utter insignificance.

Winter crossings were among the most perilous of journeys in those times. Under favorable conditions the voyage typically required six to eight weeks at sea. However, entering the Atlantic in late October, the ship would have encountered head-on the series of westerly gales that always heralds the coming of winter in that body of water, lengthening the time required for the crossing considerably. No pleasure cruise at any time of year, typical shipboard living conditions were abominable. Gaining sustenance primarily from rations of weevil-infested hardtack, heavily salted beef, and beer for drink, a few weeks out of port passengers and crew alike invariably became dehydrated, malnourished and increasingly susceptible to disease. In the confined quarters of the ship, disease could and often did spread like windswept prairie fire.

Of course, fresh water was precious aboard any trans-Atlantic sailing vessel, whether military or merchant. I use the term "fresh" here only to distinguish it from saltwater. This was in an age before technology for desalinization of seawater was known. Whatever fresh water was stored on board in casks quickly became slimy with algae and alive with bacteria and parasites, often leading to extreme intestinal distress and diarrhea. This of course, further exacerbated the problem of dehydration. Beginning about 1655, in order to sanitize the water and make it a little more palatable, mariners began mixing it with 98-proof rum before consumption, a drink that became known as "grog." One-half pint of rum per quart of water was the usual mix – enough to sanitize the water without the crew becoming completely inebriated - "groggy" - on a single morning's ration.

Adding to the misery of the arduous voyage, sailing vessels of those times had no facilities for sanitation. Certainly, there was no means of bathing. The collective body odor alone must have shortly become overpowering. And aboard a small wooden ship rolling and bobbing like a cork through storm-driven swells, seasickness was universal, even among a seasoned crew. Vomit and bodily waste had to be collected in slop buckets for disposal overboard above decks. Of course, a bucket on a storm-tossed ship would have presented a moving target. Small wonder the confined space below decks was said to reek with the stench of it all.

Frequently finding themselves in the grip of the tempest, lest sails be shredded, and rigging and masts destroyed by the wind, seafarers of the time had no choice but to lower the canvas and allow the ship to be blown wherever the whimsy of the wind and waves took it. With each new gale encountered a vessel could be blown hundreds of miles off course. Not surprisingly perhaps, the most important person on board any ocean going vessel was not the Captain, but the navigator, for safe and timely arrival at the planned destination depended upon his skills and knowledge of the routes. Once in open waters away from land, often the only tools of navigation were the ship's magnetic compass, charts, depth sounding lines and educated guesswork, based upon the navigator's past experience. Accurate estimates of latitude required at least a momentary clear view of sun and stars, which in foul weather could be obscured for days or even weeks at a time.

Even when blessed by Providence with fair weather, precise determination of longitude would not become possible until the invention of the marine chronometer almost a century later in 1759. Given the technology of the age, days and weeks could pass without Seventeenth Century mariners knowing precisely where they were. The ultimate sighting of any portion of mainland America was in itself a major triumph, and the much anticipated cry of "Land ho!" by the lookout was greeted with great excitement, celebration and prayers of thanksgiving by all souls aboard. Once the coastline was in sight, navigation to the final destination then became a relatively simple task. Even so, many a merchant ship, having survived the long crossing, would ultimately be lost, dashed to bits by a storm-tossed sea against the rocky North American coast, leaving her survivors shipwrecked in a land most of which was controlled by unfriendly savages.

After months at sea, battered by storms, living and sleeping in the fetid holds of the ship, the passengers and crew of Pumerlander Kerk finally arrived intact at their destination and dropped anchor in safe harbor in February, 1663 at what was then called New Amsterdam on Manhattan Island. Despite the difficult and harrowing crossing, passage had been by no means cheap. Fortunately for present-day researchers, the Dutch were meticulous record-keepers, and some of those records still survive. Logs of the Dutch West India Company, which owned the vessel show Jacques paid ninety-seven and one-half Florins for his family of four. In the original record, dated October 12, 1662 the Cossart name has been Romanized to "Cossaris", a common practice by the Dutch in those times. Adults were charged 39 Florins for passage. Children under the age of ten were half-fare, and no fare was charged for nursing infants.

The total Jacques had paid amounted to quite a tidy sum for the times. In fact, the Dutch West India Company had paid the Indians only 60 Florins worth of baubles and beads and other goods for the entire island of Manhattan, admittedly a pittance, considering what they were getting for their investment. As an aside, over time much hay has been made regarding the "greedy" white man taking advantage of the naiveté of the innocent savages on Manhattan, basically stealing their land from them. Ironically enough, from the Indian viewpoint, the Dutch got the short end of the stick. No native tribes actually lived on Manhattan, and it was their belief no man could "own" the land anyway. The island had simply served as a common neutral ground for tribes to gather and conduct trade amongst themselves. In "selling" Manhattan to these strange white men, the tribes believed the joke was entirely on the Dutch. The 60 Guilders in goods paid them by the Dutch basically amounted to protection money.

In spite of the cost of the voyage, the Cossart family was relatively well-to-do, and the promise of a free life, money to be made and land to be acquired in a bountiful and opportunity-filled New World was compelling. Based upon what they had heard of the New World, the storm-tossed desperate journey was well worth the cost and the risk they undertook. In fact, the Dutch West India Company had looked upon the Huguenots, the Puritans and other groups like them as a prime demographic to target in their advertisements, aggressively marketing New Netherlands to them. Generally acknowledged as the first poet of the New World, Jacob Steendam lauded the Eden that awaited the immigrants in his 1661 poem, "In Praise of New Netherland", which appeared in a Dutch West India Company advertising brochure in Holland. Perhaps it was advertising such as this that ultimately convinced the Cossarts and their traveling companions to embark on their long journey to the New World.

"The birds obscure the sky, so numerous in their flight;
The animals roam wild, and flatten down the ground;
The fish swarm in the water and exclude the light;
The oysters there, than which none better can be found;
Are piled up, heap upon heap, till islands they attain;
And vegetation clothes the forest, mean and plain.

...a living view does always meet your eye,
Of Eden, and the promised land of Jacob's seed;
Who would not, then, in such a formed community,
Desire to be a Freeman; and the rights decreed,
To each and every one, by Amstel's burgher lords,
T'enjoy? And treat with honor what their rule awards?"

The mention of "heaps" of oyster shells by Steendam is not insignificant. Oysters were not only a nutritious, high-protein food source; their shells were a prized commodity. Ground up they were used for their lime content in making durable, high-quality mortar for Dutch stone houses. Steendam's message: The New World, and specifically New Amsterdam, would provide all the resources and riches the hopeful immigrant could possibly dream of or ask for – all the necessities of life were there in abundance for the taking! One only needed to get there. The following from the Ponna Archives [15] further describes what drove the Cossarts and others like them to leave their homes to seek a better life in the New World.

"Not alone Hollanders came to America in this noble communion. With them were joined a large number of Frenchmen. Holland, in the latter half of the seventeenth century, offered the most open asylum on the continent of Europe for the persecuted, and for that reason, and also because it was "near to flee to", Huguenots from all parts of France sought its shelter. They were eager to cross the line which divided their fair fields and rich vineyards, spoiled by the depotism of Louis the Fourteenth, from the marshes precariously kept from the salt sea, but happy under the gentle rule of the Princess of Orange. But the majority of such, and thousands besides of her own people, found Holland not a country to stay in. The new world beyond the sea promised better. Westward, Ho! was the cry of the time. The shores of that most beautiful river, which Hendrick Hudson had discovered, had every attraction: and vessel after vessel left Amsterdam – (the Mayflower sailed from Amsterdam) - thronged with pilgrims, and especially to New Amsterdam - New York, the term was to become - bearing Dutch and French pilgrims: these like their puritan neighbors, saying plainly that they sought a better country, both in this world and beyond."

"The Mayflower in Plymouth Harbor" William F Halsall

CHAPTER THREE - THE NEW WORLD

Not long after their arrival in the New World the Cossarts presented their letter of introduction from the mother church in Holland and joined the Dutch Reform Church of New Amsterdam on April 1, 1663. One of the most populous cities in the entire world today, at the time of the Cossarts arrival, New Amsterdam was but a village of about 1400 souls. There was an earthen walled fort, a church, a Governor's mansion and about 200 crude homes in the community.

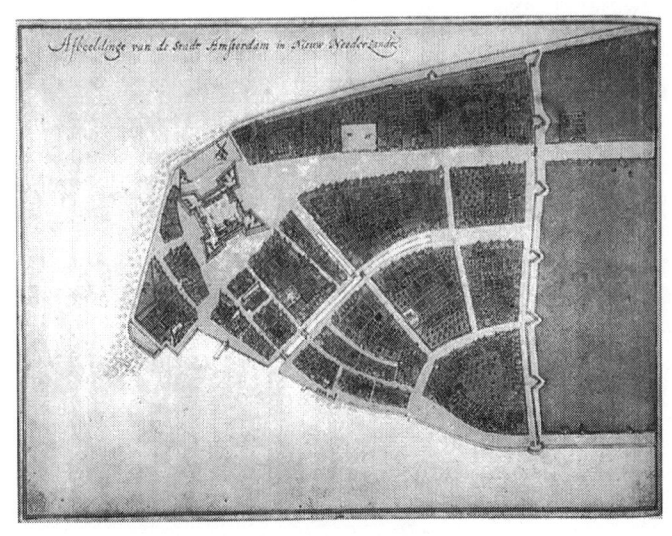

Bounded on the west by the Hudson River and on the east by the East River, the town spread out from Fort Amsterdam at the tip of the island to the palisades guarding the town's northern front. In the 1660 Castello Plan map above North is to the right. Today's "Broadway" is easily recognizable on this map, and "Wall Street" obviously was the road that ran the length of the defensive palisades, which were later replaced by a wall, from riverfront to riverfront. Beyond the residences the neatly laid out and well-kept fields and orchards (the bouweries) that fed the community stretched to the palisades on the town's northern boundary. Canals transported goods between the interior of the colony and the shipping docks on the East River.

In March Jacques Cossart and six other of his traveling companions requested from the Governor, a land grant, seed grain and provisions enough for six months. The following text was excerpted from New York Colonial Manuscripts, Vol. 10, Part 2, p. 49 [73] and is translated from the original Dutch script.

"19 March, 1663: "To the Hon. Director General and Council of New Netherlands.

Show with due reverence and respect to your Honorable Worships, Nicollas Dupuij, Gedeon Merlet, Arnold Dutroij, Jacques Cossart, Louijs Laakman, Jacob Kolf, and Jean Le Cancelier, that the supplicants while in Holland, by the advice of some gentlemen there as well as by the reading of the printed New Netherland conditions were urged and moved to betake themselves with their whole families to these regions, in the hope that your Hon. Worships agreeable to the aforesaid New Netherland conditions would come to their assistance. The supplicants address themselves therefore to your Hon. Worships with the humble request that you may please to assigne and grant them suitable lands and also to furnish them with seed grain and necessary provisions for six months, in order that they, the supplicants, may exert their industry and zeal without obstruction in the cultivation of the land, not only for their personal benefit, but also for the welfare and the good of the whole country, expecting to behave and conduct themselves in such manner that they will hereafter be able to make good and repay with thanks all that has thus far been advanced to them and what they may expect from your Honors' usual benevolence.

This doing they remain
Your Hon. Worships' servants,
Nicolas du puis

gedeon merlet
Arnoult du toict
Jacque cossart
Louis Lacqueman
Jacob Kolver
Jean Le concilie"

The request was granted, and in due course Jacques made good on the opportunity, repaying in full his debt to the Governor and colony. Colonial records show the first American Cossarts in 1667 purchased land and made their home at the corner of Whitehall and Marketfield Streets, the very site where the New York Produce Exchange now stands near lower Broadway. In fact, today it is said the main elevator shaft for the Exchange was once the water well of Jacques and Lea Cossart and their family. The illustration below is from Hemstreet's The Story of Manhattan [28], showing a typical Dutch house in Manhattan in the year 1668. The Cossart's home may have looked very much like this one.

Though migrants were required to pay their own passage to the New World, once there, grants of land appear to have been practically automatic, which was of course, a huge incentive to risk the perilous trip. As one would assume from the aforementioned advertising brochure for New Netherlands, it was in the Dutch West India Company's interest to recruit new colonists to develop and harvest the bounty of the land to which they had laid claim. Even so, receiving such a grant from the Governor was an auspicious beginning, and a bright future in the Dutch colonies of the New World seemed assured for Jacques and his family. In fact, for them and the other immigrants the promise of New Netherlands had seemed virtually limitless.

However, unbeknown to the new arrivals, Dutch colonialism in America was nearing its end. The year of the Cossart's immigration brought with it several dark omens to New Netherlands. The Hudson Valley was hit by a series of earthquakes from February through August, and the river, overflowing its banks, ruined the crops. A Smallpox epidemic struck the colony, resulting in great suffering and many deaths, and an Indian uprising in the upper Hudson resulted in the greatest massacre of whites in the history of the colony. But in the year following, the greatest upheaval and change to life in New Netherlands would be brought about not by nature or conflict with the native tribes, but by the avarice of other white men.

The Dutch colonies of the Hudson, guarded by New Amsterdam formed a wedge between New England and the British colonies of the south. The British aimed to unite them. King Charles II found ways to rationalize his aggression against the Dutch colony, claiming the landing of the Pilgrims at Plymouth, Massachusetts (refugees who ironically enough were fleeing oppression in England) had somehow given the British Crown first claim and title to all lands from that point south.

In Knickerbockers History of New York [21], Washington Irving wrote, "The result of all these rumors and representations was a sudden zeal on the part of his Majesty Charles the Second for the safety and well-being of his transatlantic possessions, and especially for the recovery of the New Netherlands, which Yankee logic had, somehow or other, proved to be a continuity of the territory taken possession of for the British Crown by the pilgrims when they landed on Plymouth Rock, fugitives from British oppression. All this goodly land thus wrongfully held by the Dutchmen, he presented, in a fit of affection, to his brother the Duke of York, a donation truly royal, since none but great sovereigns have a right to give away what does not belong to them. That this munificent gift might not be merely nominal, his Majesty ordered that an armament should be straightway despatched to invade the city of New Amsterdam by land and water, and put his brother in complete possession of the premises."

Despite the British rationalizations and talk of rightful ownership, the fact is, the motivation for their king's aggression was nothing more than naked greed. The choice port of New Amsterdam, ideally situated guarding the entrance to several great inland waterways, was a source of immense wealth to its owners. The location provided easy access to the lucrative fur trade of the Hudson, Delaware and Connecticut River valleys, and American fur and timber were in great demand in Europe, and commanded premium prices. One would assume the prize New Amsterdam represented would be jealously guarded and vigorously defended by the Dutch. Though the fortifications they had erected provided an effective defense against the crude weapons of native tribes, the earthen wall and log stockade of New Amsterdam was no match for the naval artillery of the times.

While away on a diplomatic mission to Boston, engaged in negotiations ostensibly aimed at enhancing peace and cooperation between the British and Dutch colonies, and in spite of prior reassurances from the Dutch West India company the British intended no harm with their advancing fleet of warships, Governor Stuyvesant divined their true intent and comprehended the imminent danger. Alarmed, he dispatched an urgent message to New Amsterdam warning of the impending threat and directed the council make preparations and place the town on a war footing. The old burghers of the council, however, not accustomed to action, but more to windy debate and bluster could not come to agreement on what actions best be taken to prepare.

"Thus did this venerable assembly of sages lavish away their time, which the urgency of affairs rendered invaluable, in empty brawls and long-winded speeches, without ever agreeing, except on the point with which they started, namely, that there was no time to be lost, and delay was ruinous. At length, St. Nicholas taking compassion on their distracted situation, and anxious to preserve them from anarchy, so ordered, that in the midst of one of their most noisy debates on the subject of fortification and defence, when they had nearly fallen to loggerheads in consequence of not being able to convince each other, the question was happily settled by the sudden entrance of a messenger, who informed them that a hostile fleet had arrived, and was actually advancing up the bay!" [21]

So it came about, a brief eighteen months after the Cossarts' arrival in the New World, in August, 1664, although Holland and Great Britain were not officially at war at the time, three British warships carrying 500 troops under command of Colonel Richard Nicholls appeared in the waters off Manhattan Island. With cannons armed, they turned broadsides to the town, anchored and sent a party of officers ashore to demand the town's surrender. Meanwhile, companies of British troops and their colonial mercenaries were set ashore in preparation for a ground assault.

Having come to the New World anticipating a better life than the one they had left, this turn of events of course caused a huge stir amongst the people of New Amsterdam and surely raised a good deal of uncertainty and fear for the future of their families. The British show of force was highly effective. When the armed threat actually materialized before them, what had initially been bold, defiant talk of resistance and militant saber-rattling in the streets and taverns suddenly metamorphosed to talk of capitulation by much of the populace. The people of New Amsterdam fully understood the threat represented by the British naval guns. They also understood the British Regulars were well-trained, well disciplined soldiers, and though they had much to fear from them, their Colonial mercenaries, long jealous and often hostile rivals of the Dutch on Manhattan, would be a completely ruthless bloodthirsty mob and entirely uncontrollable, once unleashed upon the city.

Stuyvesant on the other hand, would countenance no talk of

surrender. Having escaped Boston and returned to New Amsterdam, as depicted above in the David B. Scott illustration, the fiery and flamboyant Governor ripped to shreds the letter of ultimatum sent him by the British. Adamant they fight it out and defend the town at all costs, he stamped his prized silver studded peg-leg on the wooden floor and emphatically declared before the council, "I would rather be carried a corpse to my grave than give in!" Lamentably, owing to the council's delay and failure to prepare, there was barely enough powder in the fort for a day's fighting, few cannon, little food, and there was no water well within the walls. On the northern side of the town the defensive palisades were effective enough against the Indians, but easily breached by naval artillery. Besides, the town lay entirely open along the two river fronts and was therefore readily vulnerable to amphibious invasion.

If invaded in force, the townspeople would have no alternative but to retreat within the fort. Even that fallback position must have been little psychological comfort, knowing their homes would be pillaged and torched by the marauding troops. Worse yet, Fort Amsterdam itself was militarily indefensible. Surrounded by ill-maintained crumbling ten foot earthen walls, the fort was overlooked by and lay within a mere pistol shot of the hills on the northern side, over which ran the "Heereweg" or Broadway. If the fort was placed under siege, it would undoubtedly be a short and bloody one – a virtual turkey shoot for the British. The whole of New Amsterdam, including the fort, would be devastated and left in charred, smoldering ruin.

Making the situation even more hopeless, for some time, the last of the Dutch Governors had been faced with growing disaffection and alienation of the populace he governed – "Peter the Headstrong" they called him, and an aging Fort Amsterdam was desperately in need of repairs. In the year of the Cossarts' arrival Stuyvesant had written the Company in Holland pleading for reinforcements and improvements to the fort's defenses, warning, "Otherwise, it is wholly out of our power to keep the sinking ship afloat any longer."[39] Judged too expensive to implement, the reinforcements and the masonry walls requested for the fort by Stuyvesant would not be forthcoming. The Dutch West India Company it seems had been bleeding the colony for all it was worth, making themselves and mother Holland wealthy via heavy taxation of the colonists, while investing as little in the colony's defense as possible. They would soon realize the folly and shortsightedness of their greed.

The colony had been provided only about 150 Dutch soldiers, and in all the New Amsterdam civilian population of 1500, only about 250 were men capable of bearing arms. Under the circumstances many of these, who already held considerable animosity toward their fiercely autocratic governor, refused to fight for him. In fact, many of New Amsterdam's citizens perhaps even felt a change of government would not be an entirely undesirable result. At any rate, with a virtual gun to their heads, and realizing their vulnerability and futility of resistance against obviously overwhelming force, the town council, indeed, the entire population of the town, in near mutiny insisted Stuyvesant comply with British demands. With time running out and under ultimatum by the British for a final answer, the following letter was delivered to Stuyvesant, signed by eighty-five of the community's chief inhabitants.

"You know, in your own conscience that your fortress is incapable of making head three days against so powerful an enemy. And (God help us) whether we turn us for assistance to the north, or to the south, to the east or to the west 'tis all in vain! On all sides are we encompassed and hemmed in by our enemies. Therefore we humbly and in bitterness of heart, implore your Honour not to reject the conditions of so generous a foe."[37] Making continued resistance even more difficult for him, the spokesperson and chief supporter of the town council's position was Stuyvesant's own son, Balthazar.

The "generous foe" as the townspeople referred to them, operating from a position of strength, had played their cards well. Under the terms of the proposed surrender, they promised the populace the choice of leaving and returning unmolested to Holland, or to remain and retain their homes and property, if only they would pledge allegiance to the British Crown. To most of the inhabitants there was seemingly little immediate consequence in surrender. On the other hand, resistance meant loss of everything, including quite possibly their lives. Colonel Nicholls had shrewdly made the decision to yield or fight an easy one for them. It was certainly in British interests to do so, for to gain possession of Manhattan by destroying it would be a pyrrhic victory. To capture it intact, retaining its productive, hard-working inhabitants was the goal.

In fact, Governor Stuyvesant had tried his best not to reveal the terms of surrender to the general populace of the town, knowing they would be anxious to accept the offer. However, having made a copy of the British letter of ultimatum by reassembling the shredded pieces of the original, the council insisted the town be informed and overrode the Governor's wishes. The painting above, "The Fall of New Amsterdam", by Jean Leon Gerome Ferris, depicts the citizens of the town pleading with Governor Stuyvesant not to fire on the menacing English warships anchored in their harbor.

Ultimately, Stuyvesant, having been completely undermined by the council of burghers, was grudgingly forced to concede the argument to the prevailing opinion of the council and townspeople. "Thus baffled in all attempts to put the city in a state of defence, blockaded from without, tormented from within, and menaced with a Yankee invasion, even the stiff-necked will of Peter Stuyvesant for once gave way, and in spite of his mighty heart, which swelled in his throat until it nearly choked him, he consented to a treaty of surrender." [21]

On September 8, 1664, in spite of what it would mean to his own future, and in order to spare the town's complete destruction, Stuyvesant formally surrendered New Amsterdam to the British, who immediately renamed it New York in honor of the King's brother, James, the Duke of York. Fort Amsterdam was dubbed "Fort James." Thus, possession of the Dutch colony of New Netherlands, its people and its vast resources changed hands without a single drop of blood spilled on either side. New Amsterdam passed into history with a whimper, rather than a bang.

True to their promise, the new owners of the colony allowed Peter Stuyvesant and his soldiers to return to Holland. Accompanied by the sound of drums and with full colors flying, Stuyvesant and his troops marched out of the fort, boarded ship and departed for Holland. One can imagine the townspeople watching as Stuyvesant made his dignified retreat, on the one hand relieved at being rid of the Governor who had ruled over them with an iron hand, and at the same time wondering the true nature of the conqueror into whose hands they had just delivered themselves. Had they leaped from the cooking pot into the fire?

Once back in Holland Stuyvesant faced harsh recrimination and excoriation of the Dutch West India Company for having surrendered the colony entrusted to his charge without so much as a shot fired. A highly celebrated hero of the Dutch War for Independence, ultimately, he managed to convince his critics he had done his best and had little other choice than to surrender, for he had not been given the tools required to effectively defend it. Eventually he would return to America and peacefully live out his life a private citizen on his 120 acre farm, the "Bouwerie", which was located in the area of Manhattan now known as The East Village.

Though much maligned by many of those whom he had governed for his rigid authoritarian style, Stuyvesant was indeed a strong leader, and held in high regard by many for his unshakable faith in government authority and rule of law. In Dutch and Quaker Colonies in America, 1902, [30] John Fiske describes Stuyvesant thusly. "He was a sterling gentleman of the old stripe, of whom there have been many that have deserved well of mankind, loyal and sound to the core, but without a particle of respect for popular liberty or for what in these latter days are known as the "rights of man." From such a standpoint the principles of Thomas Jefferson would have seemed fraught with ruin to the human race. This arbitrary theory of government has never flourished on the soil of the New World, and its career on Manhattan Island was one of its first and most significant failures."

In Knickerbockers History of New York [21], Washington Irving tells a tale that illustrates the stern authoritarian nature that had made Stuyvesant so unpopular with the inhabitants of

New Amsterdam. While walking the streets of the city one day, Stuyvesant happened upon a cobbler who was delivering a fiery oration to an assembled crowd. Railing against the heavy taxes levied by the Company upon the dwellers of the city, he was shocked to see Stuyvesant's approach. The cobbler ceased speaking, and trembling in his shoes, awaited his fate.

Proffering a broken timepiece to the man, Stuyvesant challenged the cobbler to fix it. In a frightened, timid voice the cobbler explained at some length why he, a simple cobbler, could not repair such a complicated machine, having no knowledge of its intricate workings. He was but a humble cobbler, but there were others in the town, he offered, who did have the skills and made it their profession to build and repair such fine machinery.

The cobbler having made Stuyvesant's point so well for him, Stuyvesant replied, "Hence with thee to the leather and stone, which are emblems of thy head; cobble thy shoes, and confine thyself to the vocation for which Heaven has fitted thee -- but," elevating his voice until it made the welkin ring, "if ever I catch thee, or any of thy tribe, meddling again with affairs of government, by St. Nicholas, I'll have every mother's bastard of ye flay'd alive, and your hides stretched for drum-heads, that ye may thenceforth make a noise to some purpose." (And he would have too.)

Thus it seems even then, aversion to authoritarian rule, however well-intentioned for the common good, and desire of the citizens of the New World for liberty and a more representative form of government was guiding the destiny of the nation that was yet to be.

CHAPTER FOUR - UNDER BRITISH RULE

After the British takeover, Jacques Cossart and most other Dutch colonists, pragmatically adapted to changing circumstances, choosing to remain and affirm an oath of allegiance to the British Crown, which read as follows. "You doe sweare by the name of the Almighty God that you and every of you will bee true Subjects to the King of Great Brittaine ; and will obey all such comandements as you Shall receive from his Majestie his Royall Highnesse James Duke of Yorke and Such Governours and Officers as from time to time are appointed over you by his authority and none other, whilst you Live in any of his Majesties Territoryes. So helpe you God." [19]

As refugees from religious and political persecution in France, thus far the American Cossarts had been transient residents of Belgium, Bavaria, Holland and New Netherlands. Now they suddenly found themselves subjects of Great Britain. Happily, the change of ownership of the colony proved to be no impediment to Jacques' success in the New World. In fact, under British rule the community thrived, and the inhabitants prospered anew, having been relieved of the heavy tax burden levied on them by Stuyvesant and the Dutch West India Company. The British it seems had a larger vision for their newest acquisition in the New World. The following is from The History of New York, 1871 [8], by John Brodhead.

"To Nicolls' European eye the Dutch metropolis, with its earthen fort, enclosing a windmill and high flag-staff, a prison and a governor's house, and a double-roofed church, above which loomed a square tower, its gallows and whipping-post at the river's side, and its rows of houses which hugged the citadel, presented but a mean appearance. Yet before long he described it to the Duke as "the best of all his majesty's towns in America," and assured his royal highness; that, with proper management, "within five years the staple of America will be drawn hither." How truly prophetic his words would prove to be.

After arriving in the New World, Jacques had quickly earned the reputation amongst his neighbors as an honest and trustworthy man, and in the governmental reorganization following the British takeover, in 1666 he was elected Treasurer of the rapidly growing City of New York. At one time his portrait hung in the Astor Library in New York City. It is now said to be in possession of one of the Cossart family descendants, having been purchased from the library some time ago. As Treasurer of New York he was responsible for collecting taxes from the public to pay the wages of clergy and soldiers. Allowed to keep 4% of funds collected for clergy and 7 1/2% of that which he collected for the soldiers, the office of Treasurer would seem to have been a very lucrative one for Jacques. On the down-side, he also was held personally responsible and was expected by the Governor to collect all that was due or make up any shortfalls from the citizenry out of his own pocket.

Eventually, in 1673 Jacques and his family, together with a group of French Huguenots and a few Dutch Protestants left Manhattan for a new community in Long Island that was called

Boswijck, or "little town in the woods." Boswijck, which had been chartered in 1661 by Peter Stuyvesant, under the British became known as Bushwick. Initially, Jacques acquired about 10 acres of land in Boswijck, which he eventually parlayed to about 40 acres. He also built and operated a mill there. The settlement that started as a "little town in the woods" was to become part of the bustling borough of New York that is now known as Brooklyn.

Tax records for 1683 show Jacques Cossart paid a total of 114 pounds that year in taxes on property and real estate. At the time he owned 2 horses, 5 cows, 1 hog and 18 acres of land. Jacques died two years later in 1685 in Bushwick. The church role for 1685 lists Lea Villeman as "Lea, widow of Jacques Cossart" and tax roles for 1686 and later list Lea in her husband's place. Lea's exact death date is unknown, but she does not appear in the 1698 census record and most likely died before that. The resting place of Jacques and Lea is also unknown, but today their bones probably lie somewhere beneath the concrete and skyscrapers of modern New York City – the city they themselves had helped to carve out of a wilderness.

Jacques' and Lea's son, David Cossart[6], was born June 18, 1671 in Bushwick, a member of the first generation of American-born Cossarts. David grew up in Bushwick and became a stonemason. David's siblings born in the New World were Janetje, born 1665, Jacques, born 1668, and Anthony, born last in 1673. Of course, his two elder sisters, Lea and Suzanna had been born in Holland, before the Cossart family immigrated to New Amsterdam.

David became a contractor involved in many construction projects in the rapidly burgeoning city of New York. He may have married into more money as well when he wed Styntje (Staintiah) Joris Van Horne of Flushing, NY on October 11, 1696. Records show he bought and sold many parcels of land in the north and south wards of the city and became quite a wealthy man. Between 1700 and 1729 he also purchased sizable lands on the mainland along the Raritan River in and around Bound Brook, Somerset County, New Jersey, which had been established in 1681.

Prospering well under British rule, by the beginning of the 18th Century, early New York had virtually exploded and transformed itself from a simple trading post and shipping port into a thriving cosmopolitan city and center of world trade. The following excerpt from Dutch and English on the Hudson, A Chronicle of Colonial New York by Maud Wilder Goodwin, 1919 [39], gives a description of the opulent lifestyle enjoyed at the turn of the century by many of the city's inhabitants, including presumably, the wealthy House of Cossart.

"On every hand were evidences of luxurious living. There were taverns and coffee-houses where gold flowed in abundant streams from the pockets of pirates and smugglers, and in the streets crest-emblazoned family coaches, while sedan chairs were borne by negro slaves along the narrow brick pathways in the center of the town. The dress of the people told the same story of prosperity. The streets of the fashionable quarter around Trinity Church were fairly ablaze with gay costumes. Men of fashion wore powdered wigs and cocked hats, cloth or velvet coats reaching to the knee, breeches, and low shoes with buckles. They carried swords, sometimes studded with jewels, and in their gloved hands they held snuff-boxes of costly material and elaborate design. The ladies who accompanied them were no less gaily dressed. One is described as wearing a gown of purple and gold, opening over a black velvet petticoat and short enough to show green silk stockings and morocco shoes embroidered in red. Another wore a flowered green and gold gown, over a scarlet and gold petticoat edged with silver. Everywhere were seen strange fabrics of oriental design coming from the holds of mysterious ships which unloaded surreptitiously along the waterfront."

The illustration above from Charles Hemstreet's, The Story of Manhattan [28], depicts the waterfront of the City of New York as it appeared in the year 1700. This view would be looking westward from the mouth of the East River. The spire of Trinity Church, built 1696, and mentioned in the above quote from Goodwin's book can be seen in the left portion of the illustration just to the right of the flag flying over Fort James. The palisades on the north side of the city can be seen at far right.

However, in the midst of opulence and prosperity of the early 1700's, there was also poverty and oppression. Owing to decades of Dutch trade between the colonies and the West Indies, by the turn of the century a significant number of slaves resided in early New York. In fact, as the city prospered and grew under British rule, the slave trade expanded. In 1711 a slave market was established on Wall Street, where slaves were regularly bought and sold at public auction. Most affluent New York families of the time owned at least two or three household slave servants. Although the slaves were looked upon with general distrust by the white population, under a system naively described by many at the time as "slavery softened into a smile" they were allowed to live in relatively unrestricted quarters, unlike the rigidly controlled slaves on the tobacco plantations of the South.

On April 6, 1712 a slave rebellion took place in which a number of whites were killed and injured. Some 27 slaves in rebellion against their masters gathered in an orchard armed with guns, hatchets, swords and hoes. In the middle of the night they broke windows and set fire to some buildings in the heart of the city, then lay in wait. When the unsuspecting townsmen came running to battle the blaze they were set upon and attacked by the slaves. On a bloody urban slaughter field nine colonists were shot, beaten or hacked to death, and another six were grievously wounded.

"New York, April 7, 1712 – Some Corminton negro slaves to the number of 25 or 30 and 2 or 3 Spanish Indians, having conspired to murder all the Christians here, and by that means thinking to obtain their freedom, about 2 O'clock in the morning put their bloody design into execution and setting fire to a house they stood prepared with arms to kill everybody that approached to put out, and accordingly murdered following persons that were running to the fire, Viz., Adrian Hoogland, Adrian Beckman, son of Geradus, merchant (stabbed on coming out of his door and died in the arms of his wife); Lieutenant Corbet, Augustuss Grasset, William Echt, ...Marschalk, Jr., Brasier, Jr., and Johannes Low." [24]

It happened David Cossart was among the wounded. The article further states, "These were also wounded , Lawrence Read, merchant, Hendrick Hoogland Jr., Johannew De Honneue, John Troupe, Thomas Stersent, George Ellsworth Jr., and David Coseart, the first and the last 'tis feared mortally. Upon which the town was soon alarmed which occasioned the murderers fleeing into the woods, where several parties are out after them."

Lawrence Read's injuries apparently did prove fatal, but thankfully, David Cossart eventually recovered from what had been feared mortal wounds. The slaves, who fled the scene immediately after, were eventually all recaptured. Seeing no escape, and rightly expecting no mercy from the angry whites, six committed suicide rather than be captured alive. Serving as an example to other slaves who might entertain similar thoughts of rebellion, the remaining twenty-one were executed by public hanging or burning. Goodwin describes one unfortunate slave as having been "broken on the wheel." One can imagine what a torturous death that sentence must have entailed. One female slave was sentenced to hanging, but being pregnant at the time, execution of her sentence was postponed until after she gave birth, the offspring of a slave being a valuable asset to its owner, and the child having committed no crime.

I have thus far been unable to ascertain whether David was a slave owner himself, but as a member of the upper crust of New York society, he may very well have been. Either way, such a close brush with death at the hands of slaves surely must have had an unsettling and life-altering effect on him, indeed on the entire white citizenry of the town. In the aftermath of the uprising a new series of restrictive laws was placed on slaves, and laws formerly limiting arbitrary whipping and other forms of punishment of slaves were greatly relaxed.

I don't know if the incident precipitated the Cossart family's relocation, but the fact is sometime soon after, David moved his family to Bound Brook, New Jersey, where he already held considerable land. In 1713 their son, my 5th Gr. Grandfather, Francis Cossart[7], was born there, the ninth of their eleven children. Francis' siblings were Lea, born July, 1697, Joris (George), born August, 1699, David Jr., born September, 1704, Mary, born July 3, 1706, Jacob, born June 28, 1707, Suzannah, born date unknown, John, , baptized November 11, 1711, Eleanor, baptized December 7, 1712, Jannetje, baptized May 15, 1715 and Aefji Cossart Cossart, baptized September 23, 1719.

Residing now on the Jersey mainland, eventually in 1719 David deeded his New York holdings over to his son-in-law, John

Harpending, the husband of David's firstborn daughter, Lea. A shoemaker by trade, Harpending might have been stunned when he suddenly became a wealthy New York land owner by virtue of his wife's father's generosity. But then again, women were not allowed to own property in that age, and in deeding his New York land to his son-in-law, David would insure his daughter's future economic security after he had left New York. In his last will and testament, drawn up in June, 1736, he stipulates all his earthly possessions be held in trust by his faithful wife Stantiah (Styntje) until her death or remarriage. Upon her death or remarriage, the land and most other holdings were to be equally divided amongst his three sons. In the excerpt from the will below he bequeaths a house and total of 143 acres of prime New Jersey meadow and woodland to my 5th Great Grandfather, Francis.

"I give and Bequeath unto my son Francis one hundred acres of Upland and ten acres of the back part of my mowing meadow which is afford excepted and a Dutch Bible, and as far as the hundred acres of wood land. It must be Divided Equally Between George and David and Francis, and when my three sons Inherit their lands they must be an Equally Share in Building a house for David on his land, and as high and as wide and as long as the House that now Standeth on the hundred and ten acres which is afford willed to Francis, there must a Chimney Built in the house of Brick and a Division wall of Brick Between the house and the Canter and all the floors of the house must be Laid with Boards." [57]

The will goes on to specify cash amounts to be paid each of his six daughters by his sons, the co-executors of his will. David passed away in January, 1740. Today David's and his wife's graves are said to be located in the Old Presbyterian Church graveyard in Bound Brook, New Jersey.

CHAPTER FIVE - THE CHARLEMAGNE CONNECTION

At this juncture of my narrative it is worthwhile to make an exception to explore briefly a side branch of the Cossart family that is of extraordinary historic interest. In 1739, the year before David's death, his son Francis was wed to Margaret Van Nest. The Van Nest family had been among the first four Colonial families to reside in Somerset County, New Jersey, settling there in 1681 on land they themselves had purchased from the Indians.

Baptismal records of the Raritan Dutch Reform Church indicated "Marigritie", daughter of Philip Pieter Van Este, was baptized there October 19, 1719. As was the custom, the mother is not named in the baptismal record, but is simply referred to as "wife of Pieter." However, research by genealogist William Heidgerd for the Huguenot Historical Society, documented by him in his paper, "The American Descendants of Chretien DuBois of Wicres, France," 1968 [51], asserts Margaret's mother's maiden name was Magdalene DuBois.

Magdalene DuBois, daughter of Jacob DuBois and Lysbeth Vernoye, was baptized May 25, 1690 in the Dutch Reform Church of Kingston, New York. She was Granddaughter of Louis DuBois, patriarch of the American DuBois family. Louis was born October 27, 1627, the son of Chretien DuBois of Wicres, France. Known as Louis the Walloon, he had immigrated with his family to the New World aboard the ship De Vergulde Otter (The Gilded Otter) in the year 1660 from Frankenthal, three years prior to the Cossart family's arrival. After a brief stay on Manhattan, they migrated inland and settled in the upper reaches of the Hudson River at Kingston where others of the Blanchan family had already settled. Known as Wyltwyk at the time, or "Town of Good Will", it was the third of the original Dutch settlements and was nestled in a rich alluvial valley south of the Catskill Mountains.

Unlike Manhattan, which had been "purchased" from the

Indians, the land around Wyltwyk had simply been seized by the Dutch, declaring it their right by Hudson's discovery when he first sailed up the river in search of a passage to China in the ship, Half Moon, and claimed all the river's adjoining lands in the name of Holland. In the process of their conquest of the land, they had captured and sold into slavery a number of the Esopus tribe who had for centuries called the valley their home. Not surprisingly, there was bad blood between the Esopus and the Dutch, and peace would not long prevail until one or the other was convincingly defeated. As a result, life for the early settlers there would often be one of turmoil and danger.

Although a peace had been negotiated with the Indians by Peter Stuyvesant ending the first Esopus War, it was an uneasy peace. John Fiske writes "But in the very act of making this peace, the worthy Director unwittingly sowed the seeds of another war. Instead of setting all his prisoners free, he shipped some of them off to Curaçoa, and thus created a fresh blood-debt which the braves at Esopus patiently awaited their chance to liquidate. The growth of the settlements in that neighbourhood was watched by these barbarians with an evil eye. When the blow fell, in June, 1663, it was like a thunderbolt. Two villages were reduced to ashes, and the fields far and near were strewn with mangled corpses of men, women, and children, the victims of one of the worst of Indian massacres." [30]

For a time, the unsuspecting colonists had worked their fields peacefully alongside Indian squaws growing their maize and squash and gourds, which they traded with the settlers in Wyltwyk. But the blood-debt had not been forgotten by the Esopus. And the rum "fire water" eagerly sold their young braves by the Dutch only fanned their passion and threw gasoline on the fire of their smoldering hatred for the whites. As related by A.E.P. Searling in The Land of Rip Van Winkle, 1884 [14], Chapter IV, that enmity would be of great consequence to the DuBois family. When the colonists took it upon themselves to expand their settlement by beginning a new village nearby without first negotiating with the Esopus and paying them for the land, it was the final straw that precipitated a devastating attack.

On June 7, 1663, while Louis and most of the townsmen were away tending their fields, the Esopus attacked the town of Wyltwyk and the new village of Hurley. The "New Village" was destroyed completely, and twelve homes in Wyltwyk were burned to the ground. Had it not been for a fortunate change of wind direction the whole of Wyltwyk might have been destroyed. Many occupants of Hurley were killed or taken captive, most of them women and children. Louis' wife, Catherine Blanchan and her children were among those carried off into the wilderness, including my 7th Great Grandfather, Jacob, who was not yet two years of age.

In Peter Stuyvesant, the Last Dutch Governor of New Amsterdam [67], John S. C. Abbott writes of the attack, "But this awful storm of war, which had passed over their beautiful valley had, in three short hours of a summer's afternoon, converted the whole scene into a spectacle of almost unearthly misery. Every dwelling outside of the palisades was in ashes. Several within the enclosure were consumed, and the charred bodies of the dead were intermingled with the blackened timbers. Twenty-one of the settlers had been killed outright. Nine were severely wounded. Forty-five, mostly women and children, were taken captive, to be carried into bondage more dreadful than death.

A night of woe ensued, during which the yells of the savages, in their triumphal orgies dancing around their captives, and probably exposing some to the torture, fell appallingly upon the ears of the sleepless survivors within the gates. Was this God's allowed retribution for the crime of sending the Indians into slavery? It certainly was the consequence."

In the days and weeks following the attack several desperate rescue missions were attempted to no avail. The Indians had taken their hostages deep into the forest, and were holding them many miles from the settlement, frequently moving them to thwart discovery. In the dense native woodlands, without knowing an exact location, or at least the general area in which to search, it was like looking for the proverbial "needle in a haystack". As the weeks passed, hope began to fade, and Louis must have had to begin to resign himself to the possibility he might never see his wife and children again.

After three months of captivity, in September the Esopus began making preparations to migrate. Rather than taking their captives with them, they apparently decided to kill them all and free themselves the trouble of guarding and feeding them during their migration. Fortuitously, a member of the Mohegan tribe, whom Louis DuBois had earlier befriended had happened upon the Esopus camp in his travels. Arriving at Wyltwyk, he offered Louis information where the surviving captives could be found. With a well-armed and provisioned party of townsmen Louis set off to rescue his family at a place deep in the forest located some twenty-six miles to the south of the Wyltwyk settlement. Picking up the story's thread as they approached the Indian encampment, Searling describes the breathtaking rescue in the following excerpt from The Land of Rip Van Winkle [14].

"Before reaching the camp they met an Indian who well nigh put a stop to the expedition by shooting at DuBois, but fortunately the arrow missed its mark, and DuBois, falling on the savage, killed him with his sword before the other Indians were warned of the approach of the rescuing party. Proceeding now with the greatest care, they came to a place where they could look down from a slight eminence on the camp, where a remarkable scene met their eyes. The Indians were preparing to march westward, and had decided to kill their captives, thus obviating the necessity of feeding them on the journey. The wretched women and children were tied to trees, while about them were piled dried sticks and leaves showing the fiendish purpose of burning them alive.

Mrs. DuBois, however, being a woman of great piety and faith, and possessed withal, of a marvelously sweet and powerful voice, say the old chronicles, in the midst of these preparations, began to sing, partly to encourage, perhaps, her terrified little ones, and also to sustain her own soul through this dreadful ordeal. The song that rose to her lips was a paraphrase of that beautiful psalm, descriptive of the captive Jews by the rivers of Babylon, as with harps hung on the willows they sat them down and wept. The Indians, unused to such sweet music and attracted by the song, when she had finished came crowding around her, bidding her sing again, and this was the scene that met the eyes of her husband and friends as they came stealing through the undergrowth. The captive with arms tied behind her, her lovely face lifted to heaven, was singing with all her soul mounting upward through her wonderful voice, while the savages stood about her, transfixed with delight, and the children and two neighbor women who were tied to trees near by were listening to the holy words, their faces, all tear-stained, taking on new courage.

Suddenly one of the dogs that accompanied the searchers set up a howl and startled the savages, while they, thinking a large party of unfriendly men were upon them, were immediately on the alert. There was nothing for it now but prompt action on the part of DuBois and his men, for the Indians far outnumbered them, so they set up a great shouting and hallooing before making their appearance, as if twice their number were there, and the savages immediately rushed off to save themselves in the wilderness. Cutting hastily the cords that bound the captives, they dashed away, and the poor frightened wretches fancying themselves surprised by other savages dashed after their cruel captors in a panic. DuBois, however, soon overtook his wife and children, and great indeed was the joy of that deliverance. The poor woman's stout heart gave out at last, and she swooned away in her husband's arms."

Well, who could blame her swooning, after narrowly escaping such an excruciatingly painful and horrifying death for her and her children? Of course over the ages, this story has become legend, and some historians question the veracity of the details. Realistically, one must acknowledge in the telling and retelling, this romantic tale may have become somewhat "embellished" over time. Even so, it is known the capture and daring rescue of Louis' wife Catherine Blanchan DuBois and her children from the Esopus tribe did indeed take place and is supported by surviving historical documents.

According to Baird in Huguenot Migration to America [18], the account of Louis dispatching the Indian as the rescuers approached the encampment may be made more credible by a journal entry made after the rescue mission by Captain Krygier who had commanded the party.

"Louis, the Walloon, went to-day to fetch his oxen, which had gone back of Juriaen Westphaelen's land. As he was about to drive home the oxen, three Indians, who lay in the bush and intended to seize him, leaped forth. When one of these shot at him with an arrow, but only slightly wounded him, Louis, having a piece of a palisade in his hand, struck the Indian on the breast with it so that he staggered back, and Louis escaped through the kill, and came thence, and brought the news into the fort." [Ed. "kill" is the old Dutch vernacular for a creek or stream.]

The story of the singing of the psalms by the captives as they were about to die is also supported by Baird. "When rescued by their friends, just as the savages were about to slaughter them, they were entertaining their captors, and obtaining a momentary reprieve, by singing the one hundred and thirty-seventh psalm: 'By the rivers of Babylon, there we sat down, yea, we wept, when we remembered Zion... For there they that carried us away captive required of us a song.'"

If it indeed happened as the legend says, one could call such a last moment rescue nothing short of miraculous. At the very least, their stay of execution was the direct result of their devotion to their faith - a faith that in fact sustained many a Huguenot through the trials and travails of daily life in a dangerous land and time. It is a sobering thought to me, if not for that brief reprieve forestalling their deaths, the tender young life of Jacob DuBois would have been cut short, the river of life through the continuum diverted, and I and my offspring would never have been.

Louis DuBois died June 23, 1693 in Kingston, but during his lifetime he also led a party of Huguenots to found the town of New Paltz. When he first laid eyes on the beautiful Walkill Valley during the expedition to rescue his family from the Esopus, Louis determined to establish a Huguenot community there. He and his sons Daniel and Anthony were among the original twelve patentees of the town. Having learned a hard lesson from the Dutch experience at Wyltwyk and Hurley, this time a price was first negotiated with the Indians and duly paid before they began settling the land. Rather than simply paying for hunting rights or leasing for farming, it was agreed the land would be purchased outright. And unlike the villages of Wyltwyk and Hurley, the residents of New Paltz never experienced any problems with the Indians.

A legal royal patent was later issued the settlers for the land by the British Crown. The original patent included about 39,000 acres surrounding the town, which was first called Nouveau Palatinat in memory of the Palatinate region of the Rhineland that had first sheltered them from religious persecution in France. The acreage extended from the heights east and west of the Walkill [Walloon's Stream] to the Hudson River and was equally divided among the twelve original patentees. The community was governed by the twelve in a corporation known as the Duzine. There in New Paltz, Louis lived and prospered for nearly ten years before finally returning in 1686 to Kingston (Wyltwyk.) The villages of Kingston and Hurley were later burned to the ground by the British during the Revolution, but New Paltz was spared, and many of its original stone structures remain today.

The DuBois fort, built in 1705 by Louis' son, Daniel, still stands today on historic Huguenot Street and has been converted to a museum. As shown in the post card image above, the house was built in the Dutch fashion with gable end toward the street, "that they might save the rain water for washing and that the snow in winter might fall into their own yards, and not on the people in the streets." [33]

The venerable DuBois surname is reputedly one of only two European surnames that have remained completely unchanged since the 8th Century AD. It can be shown, through the DuBois line, Louis and his son, Jacob DuBois, Granddaughter, Magdalene DuBois, and Great Granddaughter Margaret Van Nest were direct lineal descendants of Charlemagne the Great. Charlemagne, King of the Franks from 768 – 814 AD, is credited with uniting most of Europe under his rule by conquest. He was father of the modern European nations of Germany and

France. A staunch Catholic and defender of the Papacy, he was crowned Emperor of the Holy Roman Empire by Pope Leo III on Christmas night in the year 800. He remained Emperor until his death in 814 AD.

The Registrar of the highly respected genealogical order "The Order of the Crown of Charlemagne of the United States" confirms the ancestral lineage from Louis DuBois to Charlemagne has been well-established and is accepted by their organization as proved. That lineage with proofs was graciously provided me by the O.C.C. and is included in Appendix I.

The DuBois lineage to Charlemagne lists many other persons of royal blood. These include, among others, Matilda of Flanders, who in 1051 married "William the Conqueror" the Duke of Normandy and King of England, and in the fourteenth century, Henry II, the King of England, who in 1352 at Bordeaux married Eleanor, Duchess of Aquitaine, Queen of France. Based upon the ancestral lineage of Louis DuBois provided by the O.C.C. and the linkage of Margaret Van Nest to Louis DuBois in award winning work by William Heidgerd and Matt Murphy for the Huguenot Historical Society, all direct descendants of Francis Cossart and Margaret Van Nest may credibly lay claim to being of European noble and royal blood, however dilute, through both the Cossart and DuBois lines. I find it awe-inspiring to suddenly discover I and my children and theirs are not only descended from the likes of Louis and Catherine DuBois, but also are 42nd, 43rd and 44th generation lineal descendants of such a significant historical figure as Charlemagne the Great.

CHAPTER SIX
DUTCH CULTURE AND THE REVOLUTION

Francis and his family would remain in Somerset County, New Jersey until 1765, and all of their six children were born there. Named for his maternal grandfather, Peter Van Este, my 4th Great Grandfather, Peter Cossart[8], was born in August, 1746. Peter's siblings were Madeline, born 1740, David, born 1743, Jacob, born 1751, Christina, born 1755 and Elizabeth, born 1758.

Although of French Huguenot origins, the descendants of Jacques Jacob Cossart[4] had by this time lived among the Dutch for more than a century. Of course, the patriarch of the American Cossarts, Jacques Cossart[5], had been born in Leiden, and was therefore Dutch by birth. Though the Cossart surname was rooted in France, Francis and his family were unquestioningly accepted in the Dutch community of the New World as Dutchmen.

Having sworn allegiance to the British Crown, the descendants of original Dutch settlers still considered themselves Dutch, living in a foreign country. Of course there was no American national identity per se back then. The immigrants to the New World did not come with the idea of becoming "Americans." The colonies were a loose conglomeration of many cultures. Like the other ethnic groups of the colonies, the Dutch believed their society and way of life was superior, and certainly preferable in their estimation, to the way of the English whose king ruled over them.

Though British subjects, the Dutch were determined to maintain the ethnicity of their communities rather than being assimilated and losing their identity as a people in the melting pot of the colonies. While not hostile to outsiders, they preferred to live together in their own enclaves, following their own traditions and practicing the religion of their forebears. It was no different for the Germans and Italians and Irish and Swedes and others who had come to the New World to make a new life. It is a way still practiced by some of the early ethnic groups today, perhaps the most conspicuous of which is the traditional German Amish.

One of the major differences between the English and Dutch cultures was in the laws and customs of inheritance. Among the English under law of primogeniture, or "right of firstborn" all the holdings of the head of household were handed down to the firstborn male heir. In contrast, among the Dutch it was customary to divide the family's land and wealth more or less evenly amongst the male heirs. But families were large in those times, making it necessary for the head of each Dutch family to acquire considerable land holdings over his lifetime in order to provide a good start in life for all of his heirs.

As a consequence, although it meant more equitable treatment for the heirs, continued growth of the Dutch community required large acreages of affordable land suitable for agriculture into which to expand. The fertile soil of Somerset County had been good farmland and had supported the Dutch well for many years. However, as the thriving community grew and matured, the available acreage dwindled, and that which was available was rapidly becoming more and more expensive to acquire. It was time to seek new lands if the Dutch customs and way of life were to be perpetuated for the generations to follow. In fact, this cultural trait of the Dutch was in no small part responsible for Westward expansion by the Colonials into the interior.

In 1765, Francis, along with two other community leaders, Hendrick Banta and Cornelius VanArsdale, were selected by the congregation to go to out to the Pennsylvania frontier and seek a suitable site for a new Dutch community. A 200 acre plot was jointly purchased by the three in the Conewago Valley, about 4 miles east of the present location of Gettysburg and 150 miles southwest of Bound Brook, New Jersey. This would provide the base of operations that would be the migrants' home while additional original lands were surveyed and acquired from the state for expansion of the new community. Francis, Hendrick and Cornelius led a migration of about 1000 souls in covered wagons to the new settlement that year. A second, larger migration from Jersey to the Conewago would come later in 1771.

These true Dutchmen who settled in Pennsylvania are sometimes confused with the group today commonly, but erroneously called the Pennsylvania Dutch. In fact, the so-called "Pennsylvania Dutch" are not Dutch at all, but are Pennsylvania Deutsch, descended from immigrants from the Palatinate region of the Rhineland and are therefore of German origin. In fact, the term "Low Dutch" was coined to differentiate the Dutch of lowland Holland from the "High Dutch" of Germany.

The journey from New Jersey had been difficult and exhausting, many of the last miles having been blazed through dense undergrowth, but the land that greeted the migrants' arrival was full of promise. "The land was forested with large areas of meadows that would be relatively easy to put to the plough and much of which would be simple to turn into pasture land for their livestock. The land was gently rolling with many creeks in the crevasses between the rolling hills. They arrived on a beautiful spring afternoon with the low sun giving all of the lovely surroundings a rose red glow. There was a feeling of unbridled optimism and certainty that they would accomplish their goal in this wonderful land of gently rolling hills." [61]

So, once established there, what might day-to-day life have been like in those early days in the bucolic Conewago Valley of Penn's Woods? Excerpts from the Ponna Archives, published in the Gettysburg Star and Sentinel, January, 1884 [15] provide a glimpse into that life.

"Through the six secular days of the week, the good Dutch

wives must milk the cows, bake bread, pies and cakes - savory pies I warrant, happily they were not much addicted to cakes, except to a certain form of doughnut, which, however, might well suffice - mind the children and sweep the house, only relieving their monotonous existence by occasionally going to a neighbors to "spend the day". The men, it is likely, gathered in small groups on wet days around Van Arsdale's charcoal fire, or at the carpenter's shop, where Demaree and his boys were usually working, and most frequently at "the store" - I am sorry I cannot learn who kept it - where absolutely everything was exposed for sale, notwithstanding the stock was small, from books, for which, except prophetic almanacs, there was little or no demand, down through dry goods, boots and shoes, hardware, groceries, all the way to patent medicines - the horse powders and pain killers of the last century, I have no doubt, justifying as intelligent a faith as those of the present. With such surroundings they sat through many an evening. Ah, I have seen it - It is not fancy, but memory."

It seems politics and religion was the usual subject of conversation where the men gathered after working the fields, or on days when the weather was uncooperative for tilling the soil or clearing land or raising a new house or barn.

"The Dutch boys and girls were notoriously good. The young women behaved with a propriety which added a charm to the freshness and rosiness of their cheeks. And the elderly people in a Dutch community there are always, as the world knows, very patterns of Sobriety and dignity. So, with occasional frolic and with much discussion of political and not infrequently religious subjects, fore-ordination and other strong meat of Calvinism being the most acceptable - discussions never resulting in a conversion, for generally all were agreed at the start, and happily the majority of the Dutch are born into the world with the right views, also would be little hope for them - their hours of idleness and weekly congregation passed away."

Most of the Dutch men were lean and spare. Compared to most of his peers therefore, Francis Cossart must have been an extraordinarily big man for the times. Citing Cossart family documents, his physical characteristics are described in an August 30, 1941 newspaper article in the Gettysburg Times [48]. "He was a remarkably large man fully six feet in height. His three sons, all large men, could button themselves 'all together' in his vest. At that time they rode in bright wagons, and he could fill a whole seat."

The David B Scott illustration above depicts a typical Dutch Colonial family, the women busying themselves with domestic chores, while the patriarch observes, contentedly smoking his Dutch clay pipe by the fire, and the children play on the floor, "laid with boards." Although depicting a New Amsterdam family, this might as well have been a scene from the Francis Cossart estate in the Dutch Conewago Valley. Though obesity is oft disparaged in today's society, the expansive figure of the

63

Dutch patriarch in those times was a sign of success and wealth – a respected man in the community.

Francis' political presence in the community was just as large as his physical presence. Following in the tradition of Cossarts before him, he took his natural place as a leader. He was elected an elder in the Reformed Dutch Church in the Conewago settlement. He also became a politician of considerable note in York County Pennsylvania, and his name is listed in the DAR Patriot Index, with rank designated as "PS" for "Patriotic Service" in America's War for Independence.

The Cossarts originally left their ancestral homeland in France seeking the freedom and religious tolerance they knew they would find in Holland. Later, they had come to America with others of like mind with the intent of finding room to grow while maintaining the Dutch tradition and culture. That Dutch tradition was one of tolerance and freedom for all men. But tolerant ways aside, I'm sure there must have been a good deal of simmering resentment for the British among the Dutch for having seized the colony of New Netherlands from them under threat of force generations before. With the storm clouds of rebellion gathering on the horizon, there would understandably be considerable division among the English colonists as to where their loyalties would be placed. But with what was seen as increasing tyranny of the British in the colonies, there seems to have been little disagreement among the sons of the Dutch as to which side they would choose in the coming Revolution.

"The Dutch were staunch friends of liberty. The struggles of their forefathers had been signal. The glorious cause owes large debts to Holland. It was impossible that sons of the Dutch and the Hugenots should not walk in the steps of their fathers. Accordingly, we find that in the Army of the American Revolution the Dutch soldier had no inconsiderable place." [15]

"We hold these truths to be self-evident, that all men are created equal, that they are endowed by their Creator with certain unalienable Rights, that among these are Life, Liberty, and the pursuit of Happiness. That to secure these rights, Governments are instituted among Men, deriving their just powers from the consent of the governed. That whenever any Form of Government becomes destructive of these ends, it is the Right of the People to alter or to abolish it, and to institute new Government, laying its foundation on such principles and organizing its powers in such form, as to them shall seem most likely to effect their Safety and Happiness."

The political philosophy embodied in the Declaration of Independence, authored by Jefferson and modified by the Convention to its final form had solid historical precedence. It is unknown whether Jefferson was a student of the Dutch War for Independence, but the principles voiced in our Declaration of Independence bear striking resemblance to those in the Declaration made by Holland in 1581 when she revolted against an oppressive Catholic Spanish king.

"As it is apparent to all that a prince is constituted by God to the ruler of the people... and whereas God did not create the people slaves to their prince, to obey his commands, whether right or wrong, but rather the prince for the sake of the subjects... And when he does not behave thus, but on the contrary opposes them... they may not only disallow his authority, but legally proceed to the choice of another prince for their defence..." The similarity between the two documents clearly demonstrates the influence Dutch culture and political thought had in shaping the new nation that was to become the United States of America.

Dutchman Francis Cossart did not serve as a soldier in the Revolution, though other Cossarts did. Rather, he made his contribution to "the glorious cause" as a political activist. In 1775 he was elected a member of the Provisional Assembly and was a member of the Committee of Correspondence. In the following year he was appointed York County representative to the 1776 Pennsylvania Constitutional Convention that convened after signing of the Declaration of Independence in Philadelphia. There, Francis rubbed elbows with Benjamin Franklin and other forward thinking luminaries to adopt the very first state constitution, creating the Commonwealth of Pennsylvania. The U.S. Constitution adopted eleven years later in 1787 would include the principles and rights originally set down in the Pennsylvania Constitution in 1776. Our Francis Cossart proudly and boldly took part in that.

Francis did not remain in Philadelphia for the July 15, 1776 conclusion of the Convention, because of pressing commitments with the local militia of York County. Once the State Constitution had been voted and adopted, it was time for urgent action. Having been appointed by the Pennsylvania Board of War as York County Commissioner, responsible for outfitting the Continental Army in his county, Francis hastily returned to Conewago to pursue the task.

Francis Cossart certainly did not serve anonymously or without risk in the capacity of Commissioner. He was a man very well known in the County of York, both by his fellow colonists and by the regional British governor and military commanders. Nonetheless, like the signers of the Declaration and others who took prominent leadership roles in the Revolution, he stepped forward and risked everything, including his life, to advance the cause of freedom and win independence from British rule. My heart cannot help but swell with pride to realize that I and my children are descended from the stock of such brave and true patriots, defenders of freedom and founders of our nation.

Aside from his political activities in the Revolution and his leadership role in the Dutch Reformed Church, Francis, in accordance with Dutch custom, spent much of his adult life acquiring and selling land. Over time, he bought and sold many parcels in the Conewago settlement. Like many other prominent well-to-do men of the time, to include many of the founding fathers, we find Francis was a slave owner. Pennsylvania Tax records for 1780 indicate he owned 150 acres, 1 negro, 4 horses, and 7 head of cattle, for which he was taxed 55 pounds, 16 schillings. The same 1780 tax records show his son, Peter, was owner of 163 acres, 3 horses and 3 head of cattle on which he paid 28 pounds, 13 schillings, 16 pence in tax. Though Peter apparently owned no slaves, by 1781 his father Francis had acquired an additional negro and another head of cattle, paying 55 pounds 12 schillings, 17 pence in taxes.

Among other holdings, on May 18, 1785, three-hundred-seventy-seven acres east of Hunterstown were deeded to him, which is where he built his dream home. Appropriately enough, he called the estate "Cossart's Dream." It was located on what was known as "The Low Dutch Road" which runs between Hunterstown and Gettysburg. It was on this very road on July 3, 1863 during the Civil War, where Confederate General Jeb Stuart's Calvary would clash with Union troops in the Battle of Gettysburg. The photo below, which I snapped in July, 2011 shows the fine stone house built in 1787 by Francis still stands and remains in remarkably good condition today.

Francis Cossart died in 1795. He and his wife Margaret Van Nest are buried in the "Upper" Low Dutch Cemetery in Adams (formerly York) County outside of Hunterstown. The cemetery is all that remains of the Conewago colony today. The Cossarts' original gravestones were obliterated sometime in distant past, but in the nation's Bicentennial year, descendants of Francis Cossart collected enough funds to have a new headstone erected. A 1994 photo from The Cossart Family Papers by Joseph A Cossairt, BYU Library, showed in intervening years the stone had been toppled by vandals and lay face-up next to its base. Thankfully, the stone has since been reset, but it is indeed a sad commentary that a few should have so little regard for our national heritage - a heritage that belongs, after all, not only to every descendant of Francis Cossart, but to every American.

Francis Cossart
Born 1713 – Died After 1789
Statesman – Patriot
Member Pennsylvania Constitutional
Convention 1776

CHAPTER SEVEN - THE GREAT TREK WEST

In 1768 in Hunterstown at the western end of the Conewago Valley, Francis Cossart's son, Peter, wed Mary Duryea, born 1749 in the village of Schraalenburg, New Jersey. In September, 1773 my Great, Great, Great Grandfather, Jacob Cossart[9], was born to the couple in Hunterstown. He was baptized in the Conewago Dutch Reform Church on October 3rd that year. The same church records also show Jacob had three younger siblings. Peter Jr. was baptized January 14, 1776 and the twins, David and Hendrick, were baptized April 12, 1778. Jacob's two elder brothers, firstborn Francis and second-born Samuel, following the Dutch tradition, were named after their paternal and maternal grandfathers, in that order. They were baptized October 23, 1769 and May 31, 1772, respectively.

By the late 1770's, with the Conewago Valley's population growing exponentially, it was time once again to seek new lands. Word had reached the eastern settlements of a vast promising and fertile new land that was being opened up in the interior West. Only a handful of settlements had yet been established there. Of course to speculators, the opening of new lands to the west primarily meant opportunity for gain by acquiring lands cheaply which might later be sold at huge profits. Much more importantly to the Dutch, there would be room for their ethnic communities to grow for many, many generations to come.

In 1779 the Low Dutch Company was formed for the purpose of establishing a new Dutch community there to be known as New Holland. Early the following year, when Jacob was a young lad of six years, most of the family departed the Conewago settlement in the company of a small group of other intrepid pioneers, bound for the Kentucky frontier. It is said by some Jacob's oldest brother, Francis, already 11 years of age at the time and a favorite of his doting grandfather, Francis the elder, remained behind in Conewago. Other reports suggest he indeed migrated to Kentucky with the family, but later returned to the Conewago.

Jacob's other elder brother, Samuel, his maternal grandfather's namesake, is believed to have died sometime in childhood, and he may have already been deceased when the Cossarts departed the Conewago for Kentucky. Then again, some researchers suggest he was killed by Indians in Kentucky shortly after their arrival on the new frontier. I have yet found no definitive evidence of either scenario. At any rate, the Cossarts in the party certainly included Peter and wife Mary, Jacob, Peter Jr., and the twins, David and Henry. Another son, Albert would be born shortly after the family's arrival in Kentucky. This suggests Mary may have been well-along in her pregnancy when the family embarked on the trip – nothing extraordinary for the times. It was just another hardship to be taken in stride, for in those times such decisions as when to begin a migration were necessarily based not upon issues of comfort or convenience, but upon matters of survival. Although winter, particularly that one, certainly would have presented less than ideal conditions for travel, in their foresight they timed their departure to arrive in Kentucky in early spring, so they might put in a crop of corn to sustain them the following winter.

One can only imagine, but it must have seemed quite an amazing adventure for a young lad Jacob's age. Departing the Conewago in February, the first leg of the journey took them from Hunterstown, Pennsylvania into Maryland, crossing the Potomac at Harper's Ferry to Mecklenburg, Virginia. Mecklenburg, which would later become Shepherdstown, West Virginia, was one of the remotest of the Eastern settlements, overlooking the Potomac in Berkeley County, Virginia. There Peter and his family rendezvoused with others under the leadership of Peter's father-in-law, Samuel Duryea, who had spent the previous year in Kentucky scouting the ideal lands for their new Dutch settlement. At least one sworn deposition taken decades later in

Kentucky seems to indicate Peter Cossart was with Samuel and his sons during that initial Low Dutch Company exploratory expedition in 1779. Others contest it, but if true, Peter would have been familiar with the route, having already traversed it.

According to Vincent Akers in The Low Dutch Company: a History of the Holland Dutch Settlements of the Kentucky Frontier, 1982 [54], the group in the initial migration from Conewago was comprised of about thirty souls. Departing Mecklenburg were the following men with their families: Peter Duree, Henry Duree, Peter Cossart, Frederick Ripperdam, John Bullock, Cornelius Bogart, and David Banta. Single men traveling with them were Daniel Duree, Albert Duree, Albert Voris, John Voris, Daniel Banta and Peter Banta. A second group from Conewago, led by Elder Hendrick Banta was to later follow, but instead, taking the river route from old Fort Pitt (present day Pittsburgh) down the Ohio to Kentucky.

From Mecklenburg the Duryea party headed south along what was then known as the Great Philadelphia Wagon Road through the Shenandoah Valley of Virginia. This road followed the well-worn migratory path used by countless herds of animals since the end of the last Ice Age, and by the first human inhabitants of the North American Continent. The "Interstate Highway" of Colonial times, it was the main overland dirt road by which the colonies of the north and the south were connected. Over most of its length, it was actually wide enough for two wagons to pass going opposite directions. The trail the Duryea group would eventually follow over the mountains into Kentucky was far more primitive.

At Big Lick (present day Roanoke, Virginia) the travelers would pick up the trail known as the Wilderness Road. At the time, the Wilderness Road was nothing more than a rough "trace" Daniel Boone with 35 axmen had been commissioned by the Transylvania Company, a group of land speculators, to cut through the dense native woodlands. This trail, blazed in 1775, followed an ancient Indian path, crossed the Appalachian Range and entered Kentucky via the Cumberland Gap. Once in Kentucky it split; the western fork led to the Harrod's Fort settlement, established 1773 by James Harrod. The eastern fork terminated at Boonesborough, established 1775 by Boone and Richard Henderson of the Transylvania Company.

Although primitive, the Wilderness Road was a path that would become well-worn, traversed by many hundreds of thousands of feet and hooves over the coming decade. Driven by an irresistible pioneer spirit, the opening and taming of the frontier was destiny for these brave souls. Indeed, it was the destiny of America. In Study Out the Land Essays, 1900 [27], T.K. Whipple declares, "All America lies at the end of the wilderness road, and our past is not a dead past, but still lives in us. Our forefathers had civilization inside themselves and the wild outside. We live in the civilization they created, but within us the wilderness still lingers. And what they dreamed, we live, and what they lived, we dream."

The image above is that of an 1851 oil painting by George Caleb Bingham depicting Boone leading a party of pioneers through the Cumberland Gap into Kentucky. As the painting accurately depicts, the trail was but a footpath and was not made to accommodate wagons. The little party had to travel on foot and on horseback a distance of about 600 miles from Eastern Pennsylvania to their destination. Forced to leave their furniture and wagons and other bulky possessions behind in Conewago, they carried on pack horses, only enough food to sustain them for the journey, powder, patches and lead for their rifles, seed grain and such meager tools and household possessions as were necessary to set up a new home on the frontier.

"The road by which these pioneers traveled was doubtless known as the Wilderness Road, which passed through the valley of Virginia, between the Blue Ridge and Alleghenies, and across the mountains by Cumberland Gap to Fort Harrod. The road was really only a "trace". No wagon passed over it until at least fifteen years later, and these colonists were compelled to journey on foot and with pack horses. The "pack saddle" was a forked branch of a tree fastened on the horse, upon which were hung all the household goods, and provisions. One of the early accounts of such a journey in 1779, describes the 'men on foot with their trusty rifles on their shoulders, driving stock and leading pack-horses, and the women, some walking with pails in their hands, others riding with children in their laps, and other children swinging in baskets on horses, encamping at night, expecting to be massacred by Indians, subsisting on stinted allowances of stale bread and meat, encountering bears, wolves and wildcats in the narrow bridle path overgrown with brush and underwood.'" [43]

Aside from the leap in distance, it was truly a leap of faith for the little band of travelers. As described above, the frontier in this case was not a westward extension of already inhabited lands, but rather an island of white habitation, hundreds of miles removed from the nearest colonial settlements and reached only by traversing a vast expanse of complete wilderness. Psychologically, it was perhaps no less of a leap than it had been for their forebears in leaving the European continent to come to the New World. The brave souls of the Duryea party were to be the spearhead that would establish the new Dutch settlement to be called New Holland. Certainly, these hardy folk knew they would face a great deal of toil and struggle to carve out a life for themselves there. But being accustomed to toil as a way of life, and driven by the dream of a utopian society of New Holland, they, like their ancestors, were undaunted by the distance and isolation they knew would separate them from the world to which they had grown accustomed. They would create their own ideal world there!

The plan was to initially join a new settlement called White Oak Springs Station until enough acreage could be consolidated to establish their new Low Dutch community. Also known as Hart's Station, White Oak Springs Station had been established in 1779 by Captain Nathaniel Hart and was comprised of only a handful of families. The nascent little settlement that was to receive them lay in rich river bottom land about a mile north of Boonesborough on the opposite side of the Kentucky River. Lewis Collins in History of Kentucky [9] describes the remarkable fresh water spring located near a great White Oak from which the station derived its name. "Not far is a spring twelve feet square at the top and one hundred feet deep, boiling up pure, cold and fresh and flowing off in a large and constant stream."

Hearing glowing descriptions of a bountiful land flowing with milk and honey as it were, the settlers certainly could not have been fully aware of the extent of the hardship and depredation that awaited them. They may have gotten some premonition though when one of the married men of their group, David Banta was lost along the way in an Indian attack that took place in the shadow of the Powell Mountains of Virginia, prior to crossing the Cumberland Gap into Kentucky. It is said his grieving wife returned to the Conewago settlement a widow. No consolation to be sure, there was already many a kindred soul in Kentucky, widows of the Indian wars, who shared her predicament. Over time their numbers would swell.

Finally arriving in late March, the weary travelers began integrating into the community and acclimating to their new home. Fortunately, the spring weather in Kentucky had arrived early that year, for the settlers who were already there had been facing starvation. The winter of 1779 - 1780 was one of the bitterest ever recorded in Kentucky with deep snows and subzero temperatures lasting from November through February. Poorly shod for such severe conditions, many of the settlers suffered frostbitten feet to varying degree, and all became gaunt and malnourished. By the time winter broke the remaining inhabitants were teetering on the brink of extinction.

Most every grade school student is familiar with the terrible winter of 1778 suffered by Washington's troops at Valley Forge, and symbolized in historic paintings by bloody footprints in the snow. Terrible it was, but in fact, the winter of 1779-1780 was even more severe. Remembered simply as "the Hard Winter" in Kentucky lore, it is said birds and turkeys froze on their perches, and when the wind blew they fell like hail, deadly missiles from the trees. Most of the previous year's corn crop, the staple so laboriously brought to fruition the summer before had been destroyed by Indians before the harvest. The meager corn that was available was selling for as much as $175 a bushel. At first glance, it would seem someone must have been profiting obscenely from the misery and suffering of others. But in fact, there were good reasons for the seemingly absurd price of corn, aside from the scarcity of the commodity.

In September, 1777, the Continental dollar had been valued at 7

Shillings, 6 Pence, and with early successes in the Revolution by October that year it had risen to 10 Shillings. But by January of 1780, because the Revolution was going poorly for the Continental Army, the dollar's value had plummeted to 3 Pence. May that year would bring a crushing defeat for the Continental Army in the South with the surrender in Charleston, South Carolina of 5000 patriot forces and a huge cache of ammunition to British General Sir Henry Clinton. Upon news of the surrender, the value of the dollar reached rock bottom – zero – quite literally not worth the paper on which it was printed. Thus was born the old saying, describing something of no value as being "not worth a Continental Dollar!" For a time thereafter, most trade had to be accomplished under the barter system. If one had nothing to barter, one had to depend upon the charity of others, most of whom, themselves had little to share.

A century later, Abraham Messler remarked in Centennial History of Somerset County, 1878 [10], "How the people managed in such a state of things, to sell or traffic at all, is a mystery, and how the armies were kept in the field is almost a miracle." On the frontier, where conditions were most primitive, the economic suffering conspired with the physical hardship imposed by the extraordinarily severe winter to make life itself nearly intolerable. The future of the new nation struggling to emerge had never seemed bleaker. It was indeed, as they say, "a time to try the souls of men." Describing that winter on the frontier in Westward into Kentucky [53], settler Daniel Trabue recorded the following.

"This hard winter began about the first of November 1779 and broak up the last of February 1780. The turkeys was almost all dead. The buffaloes had got poore. People's cattle mostly dead. No corn or but very little in the cuntry. The people was in great distress. Many in the wilderness frostbit. Some dead. Some eat of the dead cattle and horses. When the winter broak the men would go and kill the buffaloes and bring them home to eat but they was so poore. A number of people would be taken sick and did actually die for the want of solid food."

The suffering was widespread, and as Trabue makes clear, it was not limited to the human population. Great numbers of deer, elk and other large game animals died from exposure and starvation. Legend has it at some point during the winter, a large number of animals of disparate species gathered together for mutual warmth in a dense canebrake near one of the creeks in the area. Nonetheless, all succumbed and perished from the cold. When the spring thaw came, the stench of the rotting bodies became overwhelming - so great it could be detected downwind for miles around. For months to come the area was avoided by settlers and Indians alike as a place of pestilence and disease. The stream was aptly given the name "Stinking Creek" and it still bears the name today.

How many times have I passed that sign while cruising south on the Interstate in the quiet air-conditioned comfort of my car and wondered to myself why anyone would give the beautiful little stream such a rude name? To be sure, being ignorant of its origin, it is a curious, perhaps even mildly amusing name to the casual passing traveler. To the locals who know, there is nothing at all humorous about it. Today Stinking Creek is home to some of the poorest of communities in all of Appalachia. Still, to its residents the name remains a continuing reminder of the extraordinary hardship endured by both man and beast during the Hard Winter of 1779 – 1780, when success of the Revolution and bare survival of the hardy folk on the frontier was itself very much in question.

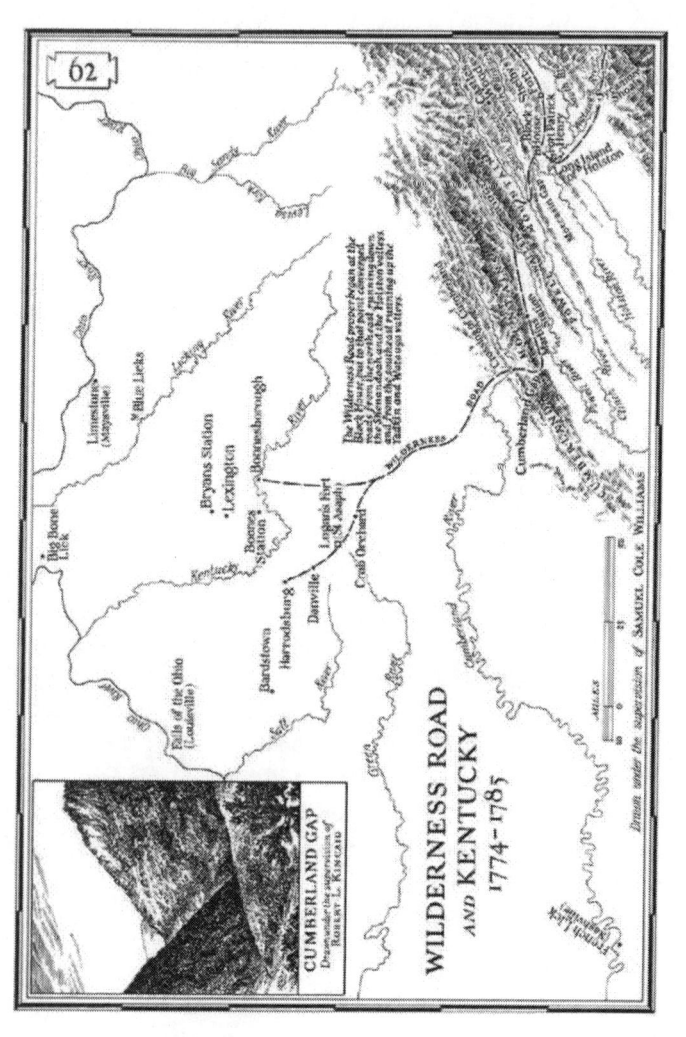

Wilderness Road Map

CHAPTER EIGHT
THE DARK AND BLOODY GROUND

The Duryea Low Dutch party was new blood for the settlement, and they must have been received enthusiastically by its residents. Insofar as there is strength numbers, they represented new hope for the inhabitants there. As soon as the ground could be worked, the little community set to work putting in a crop, which in due course by the sweat of their brows would bring an abundant harvest the following fall. Unfortunately, early arrival of spring was a two-edged sword. On the one hand, it meant blessed relief from the deadly, bitter cold. On the other, it also meant an early resurgence of Indian attacks, which had been temporarily held in abeyance owing to the exceptionally harsh weather of the winter months.

Hostilities of the Revolution were ongoing, even in the thinly settled Western frontier, and Indian tribes allied with Great Britain were to redouble that year what had already been frequent raids on the wilderness settlements. Completely unrestrained by the British, who were only too willing to take advantage of their savagery, the cruelty with which they treated their unfortunate victims is described by Daniel Boone in his journal [4].

"On the twenty-second day of June, 1780, a large party of Indians and Canadians, about six hundred in number, commanded by Col. Bird, attacked Riddle's and Martin's stations, at the Forks of Licking River, with six pieces of artillery. They carried this expedition so secretly, that the unwary inhabitants did not discover them, until they fired upon the forts; and, not being prepared to oppose them, were obliged to surrender themselves miserable captives to barbarous savages, who immediately after tomahawked one man and two women, and loaded all the others with heavy baggage, forcing them along toward their towns, able or unable to march. Such as were weak and faint by the way, they tomahawked. The tender women, and helpless children, fell victims to their cruelty. This, and the savage treatment they received afterwards, is shocking to humanity, and too barbarous to relate."

Daniel Trabue's brother John was a member of the Kentucky militia present at Riddle's Station when it came under attack, and he was on the forced march after the surrender. In the negotiations the British had promised the settlers they would protect them from the Indians if they would only surrender without a fight – a promise they were either unable or unwilling to keep. John Trabue had argued against the capitulation but was overruled. Daniel in his memoir [53] relates his brother, John's memory of the barbarous acts perpetrated during the forced march, the sort which Boone had found too shocking and barbarous to describe. "...they killed old Mistress Barger, an old Duch woman who we was aquainted with. As one company of Indians marched along, this old woman behind: one Indian behind her he would jump up and wave his Tomerhock and cut a number of capers and then killed her. The blow came when this old lady was not expecting it. They finished her and skelped her and then raised a dreadfull yell. My brother said he often looked behind to see if they was cuting capers behind him." [It is said some unfortunate souls who managed to survive the march were later burned alive at the stake once they had reached the Indian towns north of the Ohio.]

Thus, as spring of 1780 passed into summer and summer into fall, the Cossarts and the others together had to forge a life for themselves under the most trying and intimidating circumstances. Still, they never lost sight of their dream. Taking action to realize that dream, on September 25, 1780, Peter Cossart filed a treasury warrant, a "stake of claim" for 600 acres of Kentucky land. Listed in the Kentucky Land Records for Lincoln County, Book 1 [71], page 83, entry 25, the record shows it was located in the Muddy Creek watershed, which lay sixteen miles east of Boonesborough on the south side of the Kentucky River. The following entry is a crude description of that land, which had not yet been surveyed.

"Peter Cosseart assee ye enters 600 acres upon a Treasury Warrant on the head of the first Branch of muddy creek from the mouth as you go up on the right hand side of the Creek to include a Dry Spring and Some Saplins cut down"

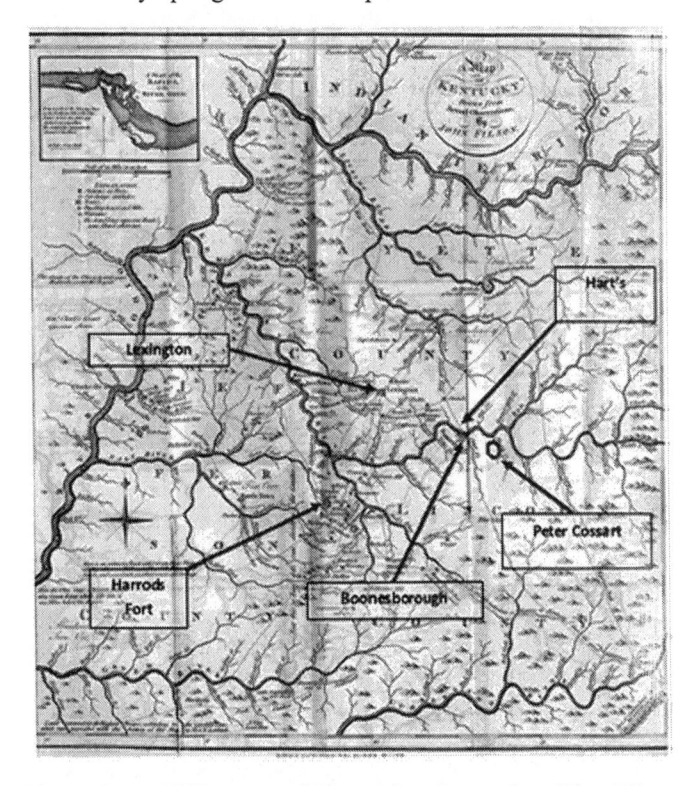

Above is a 1773 map of Kentucky drawn by John Filson. Annotations show the approximate location of Peter Cossart's claim, relative to settlements of Hart's Station (White Oak Springs Station), Boonesborough, Harrod's Fort and Lexington.

In May of 1779 Samuel Duryea, as representative and spokesperson of the Low Dutch Company had voiced to those with him his intent to secure lands in the upper reaches of the creek to build their new Dutch community, that they might establish an enclave to preserve their Dutch heritage, practice the religion of the Dutch Reform Church and speak and conduct commerce in their own native tongue. It is said, others outside the Low Dutch Company who were with Sam at the time thought his choice of land a bit foolish, for the terrain in that region was marked by a relatively steep drop, and would make farming it more difficult than on lands further downstream. In fact, today the area is a popular destination for outdoor enthusiasts, known for its seasonal whitewater rafting. Already at age 65, and considered by the others as just an eccentric old man, he easily won the bid for the land, uncontested. The others were intent on settling what they considered the more desirable lands further downstream.

However, Duryea shrewdly recognized the steep drop of the creek in that region and the swiftness of the water would make it ideal for establishment of a saw mill, a convenience the Dutch had difficulty in implementing in Conewago. A mill would facilitate the rapid growth of their community, provide income from the surplus lumber they could sell, and despite the steepness of the terrain, the soil adjacent to the creek was fertile. The new lands they would develop on Muddy Creek would support the Dutch and their descendants for many generations to come. But the dream would prove elusive. Due to the circumstances of the times, after their arrival in the "Promised Land" Peter, his family and the others out of necessity were forced to bide their time awhile.

"Brave Defenders of Fort Boonesborough" [26] was published August 28, 1898 in the Louisville Courier Journal by Kentucky pioneer descendant and historian Judge William Chenault. In the article Chenault implies Muddy Creek at the time would have been an especially hazardous area to attempt to homestead. The reason is easily understood. It was called Muddy Creek for good cause. The swift water was laden with sand, gravel and silt washed down from the higher elevations, much of which was deposited at the mouth of the creek where it flowed into the Kentucky River. The accumulated deposits at the confluence of the streams made the water there relatively shallow and a point naturally favored, not only by the buffalo and elk herds, but also by Indian hunting and war parties for crossing the river. Furthermore, the terrain along either side of the creek funneled man and beast to the crossing, and its adjoining lands were therefore relatively heavily traveled, even well up the creek from its mouth. Although the Low Dutch Company was intent on settling Muddy Creek primarily because of characteristics favorable to establishment of a saw mill, its rich soil and abundant game, the inconvenient little detail was it happened to be in the middle of a major north-south Indian thoroughfare.

Though no Indian tribes were actually native to Kentucky, they mightily resented the intrusion of these white men on their ancestral hunting grounds, cutting the trees, clearing the land and stealing their game. And though the southern Cherokee had signed a treaty with the Transylvania Company, selling them the land, the northern tribes who had long used the hunting grounds were understandably reluctant to give it up. Sam Duryea and the Low Dutch Company may not have been aware of the full ramifications involved in choosing Muddy Creek for their settlement. However, it would seem at that time, to attempt to build cabins and live in that valley might have been reasonably likened to knocking down an active hornet's nest and using it for a pillow. But then again, the indomitable pioneer spirit of the Dutch was not easily cowed by promise of adversity.

Chenault states in his article, "When an old woodsman wished to turn a hunt for game into a search for Indians, he generally went to the mouth of Muddy creek, which was the most noted Indian crossing in the country... the people above Estill's Station and at the mouth of Muddy creek were still troubled with Indians as late as 1792. A small station settled by Higgerson Grubbs on Muddy creek was deserted by its inhabitants for fear of the Indians as late as 1792." Although the Low Dutch Company had managed to raise a crop of corn in the upper reaches of Muddy creek in the summer of 1779, by the time of their return with the migrants from Conewago in 1780 several of the Boonesborough militia had already lost their lives and scalps in that vicinity.

In December of the year of their arrival on the frontier, Frederick Ripperdam and several others from the Low Dutch Company went out to further scout the land along Muddy Creek for suitable sites for their homes, bringing their tools with them. Historical references I have found do not enumerate all who were in the scouting party. Thus, I don't know for certain Peter Cossart was among them, though it seems likely he was. At any rate, while proceeding up the creek their party was ambushed by Indians. The following excerpt from Collins' History of Kentucky [9], describes the events of that ill-fated expedition.

"In December of that year, Fred Ripperdan and several others of the number, went over to Estill's Station, which was on little Muddy Creek 1 ½ miles from its mouth, and arranged with Captain James Estill and his brother Sam, to show them lands whereon to begin a station, as they rode along a trace in the cane down the creek, Captain Estill in front and Sam in the rear, they passed a half mile from the station, a large red-oak tree which they had lately fallen close to the trace. It was covered with red leaves and behind it lay in ambush some Indians, who had cut cane and stuck it in the crack of the tree, the better to conceal them. Sam Estill whose large grey eyes and almost eagle vision, nothing in the forest moving or still, could escape – espied a moccasin behind the tree, he instantly fired through the cane, threw himself off his horse on the opposite side, and shouted,

"Indians". The Indians fired too, one shot badly breaking the arm of Captain Estill whose horse wheeled and dashed back to the station. The Captain seized the reins with his teeth, his left hand holding his rifle but his horse was beyond control. A large painted-black and horrid looking Indian sprang over the tree, toward Ripperdan, to tomahawk him – all now being off their horses. Ripperdan in his fright forgot to help himself, but called to Sam Estill to shoot the Indian. Estill, whose gun was empty, retorted, "why don't you shoot him, d...n you." "Your gun is loaded." Thus reassured by Estill's voice and command, Ripperdan jerked his gun to his shoulder and fired, the muzzle almost touching the enemy's breast. The Indian let his gun fall, clutching a sapling for support, uttered a loud noise like a bear, and fell dead. The remaining Indians, fearing a still more bloody welcome, retreated through the cane. Captain Estill later died from the effects of his wound."

[Ed. Note: Captain James Estill did not actually die from the wound itself, but was overpowered in another battle with an Indian more than a year later when the poorly healed limb suddenly gave way and snapped during hand to hand mortal combat. When the arm broke, the Wyandot warrior he was battling instantly plunged his blade deep into Estill's heart, putting a swift end to the desperate struggle. Estill was spared his scalp, however. Immediately thereafter, the Indian was himself shot through the heart and fell dead before he could deliver the final insult to Estill's unresisting corpse. The battle became known as "Estill's Defeat" and being a famed and highly esteemed woodsman and Indian fighter in Kentucky, Captain Estill's death was widely mourned by all in the region.]

While obviously somewhat "green" with respect to Indian warfare, certainly, these Dutchmen were no strangers to conflict with native tribes, for they already knew the hardship and intimidation brought about by having their homes burned and friends and families murdered by marauding bands of Indians in

Conewago. A. Van Doren Honeyman states in his article, Migration from New Jersey to the Conewago Colony, Pa., 1765-1771 [7], "Some of these people from New Jersey went to Pennsylvania, and later some to Kentucky, after the Indians broke up the Conewago Colony, burned houses and murdered numbers of people. Some went to Mercer County, Kentucky and others elsewhere."

In so stating, Honeyman seems to imply conflict with the Indians in Conewago was a significant factor in the decision to migrate, and perhaps it did figure in to some extent. However, promise of virgin land to hunt and farm, and a new life for themselves and their children's children were probably factors far more important in the decision to migrate than the Indian attacks in Conewago. In fact, the Conewago Valley settlement had failed to live up to its early promise. Once having settled there, the Dutch found the soil was disappointingly poor, the topsoil was thin, overlying rocky ground beneath. As had been the case with the New Jersey settlements, due to a rapidly growing population, suitable acreage for farming was fast becoming unaffordable. Both were factors limiting the future growth of their community. On the other hand, it seemed early Kentucky had everything to offer anyone bold, hardy and adventurous enough to go there and seize it. And the Dutch in general and the Cossarts in particular had never been folk intimidated by new frontiers. To them the Indian problem was just another obstacle to be overcome.

Even so, with respect to exposure to Indian attack the early migrants to Kentucky from the Dutch Conewago Valley quickly found they had leapt from "frying pan to fire." By the time of their arrival Indian attacks were already frequent in Kentucky, and it was only worsening. Despite its promise of fertile soil, free-flowing springs, streams alive with fish, and forests and meadows teeming with game, the Cossarts and their companions quickly found life would be far from idyllic for white settlers arriving in the virgin Kentucky Territory. As spring of 1781 gave way to summer, bare survival would become their primary daily goal. Life and simple survival in the Kentucky frontier settlements would only become more difficult and dangerous, for it was abundantly obvious to the northern tribes these white men were not coming to simply hunt and trap and reap the bounty of the land, as were they. These invaders clearly intended to stay and make the land their own, and theirs alone. Without question, the Indians would fight fiercely to retain that which had been theirs by ancestral birthright. It was indeed the classic tale of violent clash between two incompatible civilizations for survival – a fight in which winner would take all.

Collins writes, "The year 1781 was distinguished by a very large emigration, by prodigious activity in land speculation, and by the frequency of Indian inroads, in small parties. Every portion of the country was kept continually in alarm, and small Indian ambushes were perpetually bursting upon the settlers. Many lives were lost, but the settlements made great and daily advances, in defiance of all obstacles. The rich lands of Kentucky were the prize of the first occupants, and they rushed to seize them with a rapacity stronger than the fear of death." [9]

In spite of the advances cited by Collins, life on the 1781 Kentucky frontier was truly life on the brink of death. He further describes the conditions under which the pioneers made their living that year. "..the Indians were prowling in every direction, stealing horses, attacking the armed companies that passed from one station to another, and killing and scalping every unfortunate straggler that fell into their hands... The insecurity of the settlers, and the hazards to which they were exposed about this period appears to have been very great. There was no communication between the stations, of which there were now several, except by armed companies. The inhabitants, not daring to spend the night out of the forts, cultivated their corn during the day, with the hoe in one hand and a gun in the other."

Undeterred, eternally optimistic, and defiant in the face of ever-present danger of Indian attack, the year after their arrival, Sam Duryea and Elder Hendrick Banta, whose group had arrived to join the others by then, asked for volunteers to go out from White Oak Springs to Muddy Creek to raise cabins and begin clearing the land for their new Dutch settlement. More men volunteered than were needed. Always a leader, a Deacon in the Conewago Dutch Reform Church, and one who paved the way for others, and already holding a Treasury Warrant for 600 acres on Muddy Creek, Peter Cossart was naturally among the twenty selected for the perilous task.

Others in the group included the Elder Hendrick Banta and his sons, Abraham, Albert, Daniel, Jacob, John and Henry. The Duryea family was represented by Peter Cossart's father-in-law and brothers-in-law, Samuel Duryea and his sons, Albert, Daniel, Henry and Peter. The Voris's were John Voris, Sr. and sons John Voris Jr., and Albert. Completing the contingent of twenty were Cornelius Bogart, Simon Van Arsdale, John Bullock and Frederick Ripperdam, who by virtue of his harrowing experience with the Estills the previous December, was certainly already well-acquainted with the potential hazards awaiting them at Muddy Creek. Doubtless, all in the party were very well-aware of the dangers involved.

Traveling in a relatively large group, this time they reached their destination unmolested. Attacking their prodigious task as though there was no tomorrow, the industry of the men was truly remarkable. Indeed, the danger from the Indians provided ample incentive to finish their task with all haste. But little escaped the notice of the Indian hunting and war parties that traveled through this heavily-forested valley, and the erection of the fort and cabins was surely done under watchful, waiting eyes. Well trained from early childhood in the ways of war, Indian war parties typically chose a time and place where odds for success were in their favor to make their move. Numerical advantage, ambush and surprise were their chosen weapons, as much as the arrow, the war lance and the tomahawk.

Within five weeks, fourteen cabins had been raised and covered, seven of which were grouped together as a fort, which they named Banta's Fort in honor of the Elder, Hendrick. With Banta's Fort complete, Samuel Duryea selected a spot about four miles to the west of Banta's to raise his own cabin on a tributary of Muddy Creek, they called "Deban's Run." Sam's cabin was completed in a mere three days. In late March, with cabins raised, Sam Duryea, Peter Cossart and most of the others returned to White Oak Springs Station to prepare their families to make the move to the new Muddy Creek settlement.

Arrangements had been made with Captain Estill to rent 50 acres of already cleared land for the purpose of putting in a corn crop, since they would be unable to clear sufficient ground at the new settlement in time for the 1781 planting. Against the sage advice of Elder Hendrick, Sam Duryea's son and daughter, Peter and Wyntje, with their spouses, Anna Shafer and John Bullock, remained behind at the Duryea cabin. The men would continue working on the cabin interior while their wives set up housekeeping. After all, it would only be a few days, they reasoned, before the others returned. Despite all the adversity, the dream at last was ready to come to fruition. But their boundless energy and enthusiasm for the dream seems to have clouded their better judgment. They had come so far and endured so much. How could they not succeed?

The women and children had moved into the cabin on a Friday. They did not have to wait long before their fortune turned sour. This was precisely the opportunity the savages had been awaiting. The attack came on Monday, before the return of the rest from White Oak Springs. Having remained closed up in the cabin for three days, their corn meal was exhausted. While the two men were outside the cabin, busily intent on cutting a stone mortar with which to grind more corn, they were ambushed by an Indian war party of undetermined number. The stealth of the Indians and the sudden fury of the attack proved disastrous to the would-be settlers.

Being outnumbered, John and Peter dropped their tools and fled for the safety of the cabin. Bullock in his haste stumbled and fell, and he immediately paid for it with his life. Before he could regain his feet, a fleet young brave sprang upon him, burying his tomahawk deep in his skull. Duryea, though mortally wounded by a rifle ball in his chest, managed to make it to the cabin and throw himself prostrate across the bed. Peter's sister, Wyntje, Bullock's young bride of barely one year, lingered for a moment in the doorway. Frozen in shock and terror, she gazed upon the scene, trying to ascertain whether her husband, lying face down in a growing pool of blood was alive or dead. Her hesitation was her penultimate mistake, and she swiftly followed him into eternity. A well-placed rifle shot pierced her heart, and she fell instantly dead across the threshold.

Being the only uninjured adult remaining, Peter's wife dragged her sister-in-law's lifeless body back inside and barred the door. Quick-thinking Anna then ran from gun port to gun port, poking a rifle barrel out of each in hopes of deceiving the enemy as to the number of defenders within the cabin. Apparently the ruse worked, for the savages, perceiving the odds no longer in their favor, withheld their charge and melted back into the trees. With no time to comfort her three terrified, clinging children, Anna next turned attention to her dying husband and shoved her handkerchief into his gaping wound in a desperate effort to staunch the bleeding. Peter, knowing the situation was hopeless, himself moments from death, bade Anna abandon him there and save herself and the children and flee before the Indians returned and pressed their attack. It must have been an agonizing decision to leave her husband behind, but one nonetheless that had to be made swiftly in a desperate situation. Anna's decisiveness and courage would mean the difference between life and death, not only for her, but for her children as well.

Carrying one child on her shoulders and another in her arms, she bolted for the trees with the oldest child following close on her heels. Knowing she dare not take the trail, lest the Indians catch them, she and the children wandered lost most of a day in the dense woods, before finally recognizing a familiar landmark, scarcely a mile from the cabin from which they had earlier fled. By this time, a dismal cold rain was falling from a foreboding slate sky, and a face stinging wind-driven sleet had commenced. To make matters worse, night would soon be upon them. Desperate, cold and exhausted, Anna reluctantly concluded their only chance to make the safety of the nearest settlement, still some eight miles distant, was to follow the trace, no matter the risk of being discovered by the Indians. Driven by adrenaline, fear and a strong will to survive she pressed forward along the trace with her children.

Fortune finally rewarded her courage and determination, for a short time after taking to the trail she met the other Duryea families with a small guard returning to rejoin the others at the cabin. Anna tearfully related the story of what had taken place there and that presumably the Indians were still somewhere in the area, pursuing her and her children. While deliberating what to do next they were startled by a war cry in the distance from the Indians, who had apparently again picked up the trail. Alarmed, the men hurriedly cut the packs loose from the horses, placed Anna and the children on them and hastily turned the party back to White Oak Springs. Spooked by the fierce war cries of the Indians in hot pursuit, the horses tore madly through the dense brush, badly lacerating the legs of their riders. Traveling through the night, however, they arrived at the fort before dawn the next day without further serious incident. Later, a larger force of seventeen men from the station returned to the cabin to retrieve the packs they had dropped and bury the mutilated bodies of the dead.

Though certainly worthy of the highest praise and respect, Anna's bravery that day was by no means isolated or unique, but was instead, common for the times. Survival and success of their endeavor in this savage, untamed land required courage, stamina and resourcefulness of the womenfolk equal at least to that of their men; faithful, steadfast, full-share partners were they, both in life and in death.

> *"The Mothers of our forest land*
> *On old Kentucky's soil,*
> *How shared they with each dauntless band*
> *War's tempest and life's toil?*
> *They shrank not from the foeman,*
> *They quailed not in the fight,*
> *But cheered their husbands through the day,*
> *And soothed them in the night."*

(William D Gallagher, 1841)

The first abortive attempt at settling Muddy Creek had ended in disaster, and no further attempt would be made by the Low Dutch Company. Further disasters would shortly befall the Duryea family, when that same Spring Samuel's sons, Daniel and Henry were killed at White Oak Springs. With four of the Duryea family murdered by the Indians, and the plan to build a new settlement at Muddy Creek in shambles, the dream for the time being appeared hopeless. Most of the Banta party removed to the Dutch settlement on the Middle Fork of Beargrass Creek, ninety miles to the northwest where present day Louisville stands. There, under protection of General George Rogers Clark's troops garrisoned at Fort Nelson they hoped to find greater safety for their families. The surviving of the Duryea party remained behind to harvest the 1781 corn crop at White Oak Springs. Peter Cossart and his family were among those who stayed to salvage the crop. Once the crop was in, they would remove to safer environs until the problems with the Indians settled.

As fate would have it, Peter Cossart did not participate in that year's harvest after all, nor would he take part in any harvest thereafter. I don't know the exact date when Peter departed this life, but according to depositions later taken in court hearings, it is well established it occurred sometime in July of 1781. Frederick Ripperdan testified in depositions given Oct. 10, 1809 in Banta vs Clay [72]: Green Clay: "where did those Durees live or make their home at the time they were killed by the Indians..." Answer: "Peter Duree and John Bullock lived about four miles from this or what we counted it then at what was called Durees cabbin and Henry Duree & Daniel Duree and Peter Cossart lived at the White Oak spring near Boonsborough" Green Clay: "which of those five men that you say were killed by the Indians..." Answer: "Peter Duree Henry Duree Daniel Duree was killed in March 1781 and Peter Cossart in July 1781 also John Bullock was killed in March 1781 the time Peter Duree was killed"

Thus, after the arduous trek to Kentucky to establish a new home on the frontier and enduring all the hardship that followed, Peter himself met the gruesome fate so many others had already met. Family lore has it, Peter, a faithful husband, loving father, and dedicated provider, at the age of 35 in the prime of his life, was ambushed and killed by Indians while gathering blackberries for his family in the woods outside Fort Boonesborough's stockade. I don't know for certain Peter lost his scalp, but unless the killing was witnessed by other Kentucky marksmen and he was within rifle shot, it seems highly probable he did.

In fact, a letter dated October 5, 1904, to the Cossart Family

Association supports this conclusion. In the letter, a descendant somewhat closer to the incident than I, Harriet (Hattie) Ann Cozart, Peter's great-granddaughter declares, "I learn that my great-grandfather Peter Cozat was killed at the old Indian fort one day when he had gone outside to gather blackberries for his children. He was scalped almost at once after he came outside the fort." [43]

Certainly, the Indians exulted in taking scalps as war trophies whenever afforded half an opportunity, and the British offered a handsome bounty for every white settler's pelt delivered them. Once dead, the loss of one's scalp would be of little consequence, except to the victims' families of course, who had the gruesome, heart-breaking duty of burying the mutilated remains of their loved-ones. But then it is also well-known in many instances the scalping took place in haste before the victim had completely expired. The truth is, white men commonly practiced the ritual on slain Indian enemies as well, as a final symbolic act of domination over one's foe and proof of the kill. The scalping knife was standard equipment in every woodsman's outfit. Stretched on sticks to dry, the grisly trophies must have cast their dancing shadows in the lurid, flickering light of many a Kentucky backwoodsman's campfire, as well as before the fires of the Red Man. Barbarous as it may seem today, it was accepted practice then - simply the way of the times on the frontier.

With Peter's death, Mary Duryea Cossart joined the growing ranks of widows of the Kentucky Indian Wars. Having six boys to now raise on her own, ages 9, 7, 5, three-year-old twins, and Albert, born after their arrival in Kentucky and still a toddler, she took refuge in the relative safety of Fort Boonesborough. In fact, it appears likely Peter had already moved his family to the fort by the time he was killed. The fort had withstood three major sieges by Indians in previous years, one of which is depicted below in "Siege of Fort Boonesborough" by illustrator

Gayle P Hoskins, which is on display in the Fort Boonesborough Museum. Only good fortune spared the fort a fourth major assault in September of that year.

"Boonesborough barely escaped a visit about the middle of September from probably the strongest and certainly the most successful of these parties, comprising Hurons and Miamis, who, under the noted Brant, had just defeated Floyd at Long Run. The Indians were urged by Alexander McKee, who accompanied them, to march against the hated fort "on the Kentuck," but the fickle and elated savages were so anxious to celebrate their victories that they scattered at once to their villages.

Boonsborough was unassailed this time in force, but few indeed were the weeks that followed when minor tragedies did not bring sorrow to some dweller within her gates or to some family within sound of her rifles." [29]

In Chenault's 1898 article [26], Mary is listed first among widows most frequently mentioned in historical records of Boonesborough. "The widows living at the fort were numerous in proportion to its population. Only a part of them are known to the writer. Those most frequently mentioned in records at command are Mrs. Peter Cosshort, Mrs. Benjamin White, Mrs. John South, Mrs. Richard Calloway, Mrs. Nathaniel Hart and a few others." The records of which Chennault speaks would make for most interesting reading and a valuable addition to this narrative, should anyone care to pursue further research on the subject of the widows of Boonesborough. Indeed, it is the intent of this writer to do so.

After Peter's death, his widow and children would pass their days and nights largely within the confines of Boonesborough's stockade. As shown in this illustration from G.W. Rank's

Boonesborough, 1901 [29], with the entire grounds of the compound occupying only about 200 feet by 120 feet, it must have seemed as much a prison as a refuge. But such a confined existence had become an absolute necessity of survival on the frontier, and the survivors would find the hardships of 1780 and 1781 had been but a prelude of things to come. The year of 1782 was to become known as Kentucky's "Year of Blood" and the land so coveted by the early settlers would more than live up to the ancient ominous name long before given it by the Indians, "Kain-Tuh-Kee" - the Dark and Bloody Ground.

CHAPTER NINE - THE YEAR OF BLOOD

Banta's group, which had initially removed to Beargrass Creek, later again relocated, this time south to a point a few miles below Harrod's Fort. There they rented a patch of land from Captain James Harrod. They were later joined by many of the survivors of the Duryea party. However, living conditions there below Harrods Fort were no better than they were at Fort Boonesborough. The land available for rental from Captain Harrod was insufficient for so many, and much of the rich virgin Kentucky acreage that lay unused was tied up in legal disputes among bickering land speculators. With both the Duryea and Banta parties residing there and no space into which to expand, the stockade became severely overcrowded, and disease ran rampant among the people. What had once been a dream of Utopia had evolved into a nightmare.

One can imagine, given the constant threat posed by Indians lurking outside the stockade waiting to take their lives, even the practical issues of waste and trash removal from the badly overcrowded compound would quickly become problematic. The traditionally fastidiously clean Dutch were forced to live in squalor and filth. Theodore M Banta in Conquest of a Continent [61] declares, "This period at the Dutch station below Harrod's Fort was the most distressful that the Dutch families had endured in their long history on this continent. Many died from contagious diseases during this trying period. This was a devastating time for the Low Dutch pioneers who in the past were used to cleanliness and spotless housekeeping."

The severe overcrowding at the stations and the continually growing menace from Indian war parties made life in Kentucky simply unbearable for many. In The Fighting Frontiersman - The Life of Daniel Boone [45], John Bakeless says of the year 1782, "One blow after another fell, now here, now there, until the more timid settlers again packed up for departure and Daniel

Boone himself was on the verge of despair... By August the Indians were everywhere."

That year ever increasing numbers of white settlers would be slain by Wyandot, Delaware, Cherokee, and Shawnee Indian war parties, encouraged to murder by the British, whom the Indians counted as allies. To keep the Indian tribes of the New World placated and reduce the need to maintain large numbers of British troops in the colonies, King George in the Proclamation of 1763 had prohibited any and all Colonial settlement on lands west of the Appalachian range. At the outbreak of the War for Independence, many tribes had initially attempted to remain neutral in what they saw as the White Man's Civil War. However, it soon became obvious they would be forced to choose sides to protect their own tribal interests. With George having taken such a position in his Proclamation, it's not hard to understand why most Indian tribes eventually threw in their lot with the British when the Revolution erupted, rather than with the colonists.

Also, the temptation of booty and glory in war proved irresistible to the younger, more impetuous of Indian braves. In the Treaty of Point Pleasant the northern tribes under the moderate Shawnee Chief Cornstalk had agreed to remain north of the Ohio. Despite the treaty, "British presents and British influence were too powerful with the fickle Indian tribes, the younger portions of which were always but too ready to be enticed into war, when the double prospect of glory and plunder was glitteringly held out before them." [60]

Ironically enough, aside from the well-known issues of "taxation without representation" the prohibition of Westward expansion in the Proclamation of 1763 contributed to a great degree to the rising discontentment among the colonists, which discontentment eventually led to Revolution. In retribution for their insolence in defying the will of the Crown and settling in

Kentucky, many a white settler's scalp would be lifted by tomahawk, men, women and children taken as Indian slaves, and homes and forts burned to the ground with the full approval, encouragement, and indeed, as we have already seen, under the leadership and direction of British commanders. In July of 1782 the British led the largest war party of Wyandot warriors, about 500 strong, ever to enter Kentucky from Ohio.

As the death toll rose in the Year of Blood, many of Peter Cossart's compatriots would share the untimely fate he had met. Collins writes, "These Pennsylvanians were good Soldiers and good Citizens, but their unfamiliarity with Indian warfare methods cost many of them their lives, it is shown of all the areas these Dutchmen settled, Kentucky was the costliest for them in human life." Speaking specifically of the community of White Oak Springs Station he writes, "The settlers were composed principally of families from Pennsylvania – orderly, respectable people, and the men good soldiers. But they were unaccustomed to Indian warfare, and the consequence was that, of some ten or twelve men, all were killed but two or three." [9]

Colonel Richard Henderson, founder and chief promoter of the Transylvania Company, names many of those living at White Oak Springs and describes the extent of depredation wrought on them by the Indians. "Hart's Station, at White Oak Spring, located in the Kentucky River bottom about one mile above Boonesborough, had been settled in 1779 by Nathaniel Hart and others, and here a small fort was built. The principal persons who lived at this fort were Nathaniel Hart's family, Lawrence Thompson's family, Henry Duree, Albert Voris, Daniel Duree, John Banta, Samuel Duree, Frederick Ripperdan, Peter Cosshort, and Paul Banta. Many of them were killed by Indians soon after coming to the country. Hart's Station in 1782, with perhaps one hundred souls in it, was reduced in August to three fighting men. This was the period when Bryant's Station was also besieged." [3]

Even the founder of the White Oak Springs settlement, Captain Nathaniel Hart, a man certainly not unfamiliar with Indian warfare, himself fell prey to the Indians on July 22, 1782, ambushed while riding his horse through the woods outside Boonesborough. The following letter, complete with grammatical and punctuation errors and misspellings, was written by Jesse Benton to Nathaniel's brother, Thomas Hart, back in North Carolina, confirming Nathaniel's death.

"Your brother Nat. Hart, our worthy & respected friend; I doubt is cutt off by the savages, at the time, & in the manner, as first represented, to wit, that he went out to hunt his horses, in the Month of July or Augt. it is supposed the Indians in ambuscade, betwixt Boonsbo. & Knockuckle, intended to take him prison, but killd. his horse & at this same time broke his thigh, that the savages finding their prisoner with a thigh broken, was under necessity of puting him to death by shooting him through the heart, at so small a distance as to powder burn his flesh. He was Tom-Hawked, Scalped & lay two days before he was found & buried. This account has come by difrent hands, & confirmed to Col. Henderson by a letter from an intimate friend of his at Kenruck"

As is so graphically illustrated in the above missive, by the summer of '82 it had become nearly impossible for the settlers to tend their stock and crops, or even to collect drinking water from the springs and food from fields and forest. For venturing outside the stockade compound of the forts, even in light of day, was a huge gamble in those times, and the Indians were constantly on the prowl, looking to take scalps and whatever booty they could lay hands on. Bakeless records, "...at Estill's Station they caught a young girl outside the stockade and gleefully killed her within sight of the fort."[45] Collins in History of Kentucky [9] describes the killing of the girl, which took place in March of 1782, in more grim detail.

"One of the most painful incidents of the war was the murder at this station of Miss Jennie Gass, who went out early in the morning to milk the cows, and while her mother, who saw the Indians, cried from the station, "run, Jennie, run, the Indians are coming," her murderers, in mockery of the mother, jumped upon a log and shouted in response, "run, Jennie, run."

Easily catching up to the fleeing girl, the savages killed and scalped poor young Jennie on the spot with her helpless mother looking on in horror. At the time of this incident, it seems all the able-bodied fighting men of the fort were away in pursuit of another band of Indians. Receiving word by boy courier of the atrocity that had been perpetrated against his station, Captain Estill immediately turned his party of 25 militia soldiers in pursuit of the retreating Wyandot war party, which happened to be of equal number. It was when they caught up and engaged the Indians, that Captain Estill met his fate as already described above in the battle known as "Estill's Defeat." When telling of the August 1782 siege at Bryant's Station, mentioned above by Henderson, Bakeless writes, "The bodies would lie out there in the cleared space, the watching husbands knew, the long-haired scalps safe only so long as rifles enough still spoke from the loopholes to keep the scalping knives away from the dead." [45]

What frightening, violent, hair-raising times (literally) in which to have lived! What courage and steely resolve it demanded of the pioneers, both men and women, determined to see it through! Notes from Daniel Boone's journal reflect his own frustration and discouragement in the face of the constant harassment from the Indians. "Our affairs became more and more alarming. Several stations which had lately been erected in the country were continually infested with Indians, stealing their horses and killing the men at every opportunity. In a field, near Lexington, an Indian shot a man, and running to scalp him, was himself shot from the fort, and fell dead upon his enemy." [4]

Still, the war in the Colonies had been a long and costly one for Great Britain, and political pressure had long been mounting from within to disengage from what had become a quagmire for them. Continuing bloodshed in the frontier notwithstanding, the surrender of British General Cornwallis at Yorktown, Virginia in October of 1781 had been a major defeat for them and signaled the beginning of the end for the British dominion over the Colonies. By November in the Year of Blood, peace negotiations were begun in Washington. The protracted war was sapping far too much from British national coffers, and at last, the once seemingly invincible Great Britain informed America she would be granted her independence. The Motherland had apparently reached the bitter, but pragmatic conclusion maintaining discipline among her unruly children and retaining her colonies by force was simply costing much more than it was worth to the British Empire, both in terms of Pounds Sterling and in the currency of blood. The ultimate decision by the Crown to bow out of the war more or less left Britain's Indian allies in America "holding the bag."

The same month peace negotiations got under way Boone, with a contingent of men from Boone's Station and surrounding settlements, followed General George Rogers Clark into Ohio, where the Indian alliance, having been abandoned by their former British allies, was convincingly defeated, their villages burned and their crops laid waste. The long awaited retribution delivered their hated Indian tormentors instilled a new sense of optimism among the Kentucky settlers, who by that time had been thoroughly demoralized by the hardships they had suffered over the years. Although the Indian wars would continue until 1794 in Ohio, Indiana, and Illinois Territories, and sporadic Indian attacks still took place in Kentucky, finally, after the long bloodbath, a period of relative peace ensued for a time in Kentucky.

A peace treaty was signed in Paris the following spring. Later that year the Low Dutch Petition of 1783 was read before Congress, documenting in the Congressional Record the Kentucky settlers' tales of woe and disappointment upon arriving in a land they had so hoped would bring their families peace and prosperity, but instead had brought hardship for all, and financial ruin and death for many of them. A portion of said petition is excerpted here.

"That in the Spring of the Year 1780, they moved to Kentucky with their families and effects with a view and expectation to procure a Tract of Land to Enable them to settle together in a body for the convenience of civil Society and propagating the Gospel in their known language; when they arrived there, to their sorrow and disappointment they were, thro' the dangerousness of the times by a cruel Savage Enemy, obliged to settle in Stations of Forts in such places where there was the most appearance of safety; notwithstanding all their precaution, numbers of them suffered greatly in their property, several killed and others captivated by the Enemy, living in such distressed confined way, always in danger, frequently on Military duty, it was impossible for them to do more than barely support their families with the necessaries of life, by which means they are much reduced" [61]

Because disputes as to the legality of their claims arose between the settlers and the state of Virginia, of which the whole of Kentucky was but a county, many, including Daniel Boone himself, lost the land they had purchased in good faith and for which they had fought and risked their very lives to lay claim.

The court's landmark decision ruled the purchase of Kentucky lands from the Southern Cherokee Indians made by the Transylvania Company had been illegal. It was argued by the State, since the treaty had been consummated in March of 1775, before the start of the Revolution, British Common Law applied. Such purchases from the Indians by private citizens and citizens groups had been clearly prohibited by George's Royal Proclamation of 1763.

In turn, it was argued, any who had purchased land from the Boonesborough Land Office of the Transylvania Company had done so illegally, because the land was not the Company's land to sell, but belonged to the State of Virginia. The court agreed. For many a Kentucky settler the decision created an economic disaster, the magnitude of which, on a relative scale, has seldom been equaled in the nation's history. The 1783 Low Dutch Petition goes on to request a tract of land be made available, sufficient for the surviving settlers to form the community to which they had aspired when they first migrated to Kentucky. A grant from Congress would give claim to such lands the legitimacy their previous claims had apparently lacked.

Signatures on the petition included Peter's widow, who signed herself "Marya Cozart, widow." Also on the petition are the familiar Dutch and French surnames of Banta, Bogart, Brinkerhoff, Brewer, Cossart, Cownover, Cosezine, Debaen, Demaree, Durie, Hogeland, Hooghtelin, Krosen, Luce, Pursel, Saulter, Smock, Seabourn, VanArsdale, VanDyke, VanHorn, VanPelt, VanTine, Voorhees, Westerfield, Westervelt, among others. Their effort was futile, however, for Congress failed to act on the petition, simply tabling it. It would be up to the Low Dutch migrants to make lemonade from the lemons they had been handed by the court.

Undeterred, the survivors of the Low Dutch Company were eventually able to purchase 8600 acres from Daniel Boone's brother, Squire Boone, which they divided amongst themselves in lots of about 200 acres on average. (See Appendix IV) The initial purchase in 1786 of 5600 acres included 34 lots. Lot #18 was purchased by one Francis Cossart, for the sum of 43 Pounds, 19 Schillings, 11 Pence. I know not whether Francis the Elder was planning to later migrate there, or if the Francis Cossart who purchased the lot was in fact his grandson. The lands of the Low Dutch Tract by the way, were not owned individually, but were initially managed by Hendrick Banta's son, Abraham Banta, until settled up and transferred to George Bergen as trustee of the collective.

The fact is Francis the Elder never migrated to the Kentucky Low Dutch Tract, remaining in Conewago until his death in 1795. According to statements attributed to Francis' granddaughter, artist Mary Cassatt, who grew up in the house, Francis had grown so obese as to be confined to his living quarters. No longer able to get up and down the stairs, the last years of his life were spent in a basement room in the house he had built, which is where he died. [43]

Although the Revolution had ended by the time of the land purchase from Squire Boone, the Dutch who settled the land there continued to live and work under peril from the Indians for some time after. "The company members worked together, some standing guard while others labored. At night they went into the fort for protection against the Indians, closing the doors and pulling the latch string inside. The old spring that supplied the company with water is still in use. These good old people cleared the Indians from the country and the wild animals from the forest. They also cleared the heavy timber from the land and built houses for themselves, and it was long years before they could safely leave the latch string outside at night." [40]

The principal town in the community they established was called Banta Town, and later renamed Pleasureville; a pleasant sounding, lyrical name that belies the hardship faced and gutsy determination, indeed quite literally, the blood, sweat and tears required of the Dutch migrants to realize their ultimate goal. Of course, all this progress came about much too late for Peter Cossart to benefit from it. Neither did Peter's son, Jacob, settle in the new Low Dutch Tract. Along with about half the surviving Conewago Dutch migrants, Jacob instead settled and homesteaded on land around Harrods Fort. His father's 600 acres in the Muddy Creek watershed was transferred to Henry Brooks, who eventually lost the land in a lengthy lawsuit with Green Clay.

Certainly, there were many claims and counter-claims to be decided over rightful ownership of lands in Kentucky, and court suits continued for many years into the next century. Many depositions in those cases were made under oath by persons who lived in the times, and their first-hand accounts remain a part of early Kentucky court records. In 1809, Ambrose Coffee, an early resident hunter of Boonesborough, gave his deposition in a dispute between Elder Hendrick Banta's son, Abraham Banta, and another claimant with respect to a tract of 2040 acres on Muddy Creek. A portion of the tract appears to have included the land Peter Cossart had claimed in his 1780 Treasury Warrant. "Deban's Run" mentioned in the deposition empties into Muddy Creek. Coffee's sworn testimony was made before Commissioners John Barnett, John Crooke, Joseph Barnett and Samuel Gilbert.

"I first became acquainted with this Muddy Creek that we are now at in the year 1777 and with Deban's Run in March, 1779. Old Mr. Duree [Samuel Duryea], Peter Duree, Henry Duree, Peter Cossart came out in company with myself from Boonesborough. We came up the East Fork of Otter Creek to where the trace forked. Said old Mr. Duree, says he, there is Deban's Run, and says he, I gave it its name. His two sons, Peter Cossart that was with him, and myself, the other three said the same, and said they called it Deban's Run. In the spring of 1781, deponent and John Banta and Albert Bones came out a hunting from Boonesborough to Banta's cabins and killed some buffalos and returned to Boonesborough. These people, Durees and Cossart, were not all killed by the Indians in the year 1780, but I think Peter Duree and John Bullock and John Bullock's wife – a daughter of old man Duree – were killed in the year 1782, as well as I remember; but I kept no memorandum of it." [32]

By Coffee's eyewitness testimony above, Peter Cossart apparently accompanied Sam Duryea in 1779 when he first explored the Muddy Creek watershed, presumably returning with Duryea in the fall of that year to Conewago to bring his family back to Kentucky in the spring of 1780. It should be noted however, other depositions taken in the same case cast doubt on the veracity of Coffee's testimony with regard to the year of his trip to Deban's run with Cossart and the Duryeas. It is possible Coffee's memory simply failed him, and the trip he refers to actually took place in March of 1780 after the migrants had arrived in Kentucky.

Also by Coffee's account, the Banta and Duryea cabins were indeed established there on Muddy Creek and its tributary, Deban's Run, early in the year 1781. Coffee remembered well the Indian attack that took place at the Duryea cabin, which I have already described in the preceding chapter. He correctly named the individuals killed there but again, may have been incorrect about the year, of which he admits he is unsure. Later in the deposition, speaking again of Muddy Creek, Coffee confirms as stated in the previous chapter, no fields had been cleared there by the Low Dutch in time for the 1781 planting. This is a significant detail, as granting of deeds to early Kentucky land claims, even those deemed "legal" was conditional upon successfully raising a crop on the claim, or "improvement." His deposition continues...

"Old Mr. Duree, I don't know when he died, but Henry Duree and Daniel Duree were killed at the White Oak Spring in an early period. Cassart was killed at Boonesborough on an early date... ...I knew no fields in 1781. I knowed Banta's Improvement. It was up here above the mouth of Deban's Run on the bank of Muddy Creek and the Improvement where Peter Duree, John Bullock and John Bullock's wife were killed, on the branches of Muddy Creek." [The lawsuit dragged on for many years after this deposition was taken.]

The struggle for the settlements of early Kentucky was on one level admittedly a series of battles fought by individuals and groups of individuals for simple self-survival. On another, it was a fight for survival of the Dutch culture. On a still higher level it was of great moment in the Revolution and highly significant to the future of the United States of America as a whole. The Cossart family was there, playing their part in that struggle of truly monumental consequence to the emerging nation. Archibald Henderson in "The Conquest of the Old Southwest", 1920 [66] writes:

"The little chain of stockades along the far-flung frontier of Kentucky was tenaciously held by the bravest of the race, grimly resolved that this chain must not break. The Revolution precipitated against this chain wave after wave of formidable Indian foes from the Northwest under British leadership... The successful defense of the Transylvania Fort, made by these indomitable backwoodsmen who were lost sight of by the Continental Congress and left to fight alone their battles in the forests, was of national significance in its results. Had the Transylvania Fort fallen, the northern Indians in overwhelming numbers, directed by Hamilton and led by British officers, might well have swept Kentucky free of defenders and fallen with devastating force upon the exposed settlements along the western frontiers of North Carolina, Virginia, and Pennsylvania, This defense of Boonesborough, therefore, is deserving of commemoration in the annals of the Revolution, along with Lexington and Bunker's Hill. Coupled with Clark's meteoric campaign in the Northwest and the subsequent struggles in the defense of Kentucky, it may be regarded as an event basically responsible for the retention of the trans-Alleghany region by the

United States. The bitter struggles, desperate sieges, and bloody reprisals of these dark years came to a close with the expeditions of Clark and Logan in November, 1782, which appropriately concluded the Revolution in the West by putting a definite end to all prospect of formidable invasion of Kentucky."

In 1792, when Kentucky was admitted to the Union as a Commonwealth, Boonesborough was among the largest of towns in the state, and for a time it was considered a prime contender for choice as a state capital. The surrounding land produced excellent quality tobacco, a good money crop, and it seemed Boonesborough had great potential to prosper and grow. However, as the problems with the Indians waned, more and more settlers deserted the town for homesteads in the countryside. By 1810 Boonesborough had declined to an obscure river hamlet. Later still, its lonely and forlorn ruins occupied the back end of someone's farm for a time. Eventually, time removed all traces of the original town entirely from the landscape, and only the bones and ghosts of the settlers who lived and died there remained. Fort Boonesborough had served her purpose and passed into history, and civilization moved on. Still, as so eloquently stated in the introduction to Ranck's book, Boonesborough [29], "The blood that flowed through the veins of these fearless and hardy pioneers and warmed their hearts and served their strong arms yet courses through the veins of their descendants and makes the site of the old vanished station hallowed ground."

Hallowed ground or not, like many other would-be Kentucky homesteader families, Peter's wife and children understandingly became disenchanted with Kentucky. Who could blame them in light of the loss of husband and father and the continuing murderous carnage visited there upon their communities by the Indians? In years following Peter's death, breaking with Dutch tradition, his family more or less scattered. Most moved on the new frontiers, leaving the bloody land of bitter memories behind.

For the Cossarts the dream of a Dutch community and homesteads in New Holland to pass down to their children and grand children had died with Peter.

For a time, north of the Ohio River, the Indian alliance, aided by some Canadian militia, continued to resist the advance of White encroachment on their ancestral lands. However, in 1794, the alliance, no longer enjoying support of the British, was crushed by General "Mad Anthony" Wayne's forces in the Battle of Fallen Timbers at Maumee, outside present day Toledo. The subsequent 1795 Treaty of Greenville pacified the region and opened it up to new settlement. In 1796 Peter's widow remarried to Cornelius Vanhice in Mercer County. With the Indian threat subdued, along with several other Dutch families, Mary, Cornelius and Mary's sons migrated from Kentucky to what is today Warren County, Ohio, northeast of Cincinnati. Mary remained there until her death in 1800. Due to the rapid influx of white settlers, Ohio achieved statehood in 1803. Warren County was formed from Hamilton County the same year.

One of the twins, David, returned to Harrod's Fort and married Polly Banta there in 1805. In the 1820's David and Polly migrated to Johnson County, Indiana, where it is said they played an instrumental role in establishing the community of Greenwood. David's twin, Henry, remained in Warren County, Ohio and died in the town of Lebanon in March, 1853. Albert, the youngest of Peter and Mary's sons, married Magdalena Banta in 1803 in Warren County, later moving briefly back to Kentucky, then to Switzerland County, Indiana. After residing there for a time, they eventually migrated to Vermilion County, Illinois. Three of Albert's nephews, sons of his brother, Jacob, including my Great-Great Grandfather, David, would shortly thereafter follow their uncle's lead and homestead their own land there, helping to settle what was then, still backwoods Illinois.

Despite the bitter memories, of all of Peter's sons, my Great, Great, Great Grandfather Jacob, alone seems to have felt a connection strong enough to make him stay in Kentucky, the place of his father's dreams. It was there Jacob had spent his boyhood, adolescence and young adulthood. It was where his father died, and it was there Jacob would choose to make a life for himself. He remained in Kentucky or soon returned and became a hatter and farmer by profession and a minister of the local Christian Church in the Harrod's Fort settlement.

As recorded in the Kentucky Land Grants, Volume I, Part 1, Chapter IV, page 505, one Jacob Casat was later granted a plot of 150 acres on the Kentucky River in Mercer County, surveyed November 7, 1816. Despite the spelling, this is undoubtedly our Jacob Cossart. To find the surname for the same individual spelled differently in different public records (Casat / Cassat / Cosat / Cossart / Cosshort / Cozat / Cozart, etc.) is not at all unusual, especially in those times. In the 1809 testimony of Ambrose Coffee above, we see that Peter Cossart's surname was spelled at least two ways (Cossart and Cassart) within the same court transcript in testimony taken on the same day, given by the same deponent. Indeed, in the 1810 Federal Census for Mercer County, Kentucky, Jacob is listed as head of household with his name spelled, "Jacob Casat."

In the book, Kentucky: A History of the State, Perrin, Battle and Kniffin, 1887 [22], Peter's son, Jacob and his progeny are enumerated. "Jacob was married in 1799 to Margaret, daughter of Henry Comingore, of Mercer County (born March 15, 1783, died June 2, 1842), [by some accounts the year of their marriage was 1797] and from their union sprang Peter, Daniel, Elisha, Rachael (Terhune), Mary (Randolf), Henry, David, Ann (Davis), Jacob C., John and Abraham." The David Cossart[10] of which the book speaks was my Great, Great Grandfather, named after his father's brother, one of the Cossart twins.

The Cossarts and the Comingores had long been neighbors, even prior to the Cossarts' 1780 migration to Kentucky. Margaret (Peggy) Comingore's parents, like Jacob Cossart's family, had migrated there from the Dutch Conewago settlement, although later than the Cossarts. Margaret's father, Henry C Comingore, had served as a Pennsylvania Revolutionary War Militia Soldier and Minuteman for York County. Like Francis Cossart, Henry Comingore is listed in the DAR Patriot Index. He had also been an Elder in the Dutch Reformed Church of Conewago, as Francis Cossart had been. In the close-knit community he doubtless would have been well acquainted with Francis Cossart and his family, including Francis' son, Peter, and Grandson, Jacob, to whom his daughter would eventually be wed.

On the 6th of May, 1833, at the age of 84, Henry Comingore appeared in Mercer County Court to apply for his Revolutionary War pension. Supporting witnesses at that hearing were Samuel Banta and Henry's brother, John Comingore. The following transcript of the statement sworn by them is part of the court record.

"We Samuel Banta and John Comingore [illegible – possibly "Sr."] Citizens of Mercer County & State of Kentucky Do hereby state upon oath that we are well acquainted Henry Comingore Sen. Who has sworn and subscribed the foregoing Declaration, that we were raised all of us in York County Pennsylvania and we know certainly of his serving two tours as a Soldier in the Revolutionary War and that he was absent frequently and we feel fully satisfied that he served as he states in his foregoing declaration and that he is a man of veracity. Given under our hands and seals this 6th day, May 1833

Samuel Banta /s/ [His Seal]

Mercer County [Illegible] John Comingore /s/ [His Seal]

Mercer County Court 1833"

[The above transcription of the record is courtesy of Chris Laster]

In 1934 Congress directed a Pioneer National Monument be established at the site of Boonesborough honoring those who died in the fighting there and at surrounding settlements, including White Oak Springs Station, and at the Battle of Blue Licks in the closing days of the Revolution. My Great, Great, Great, Great Grandfather, Peter Cossart, is among the brave, hardy pioneers listed on the monument there who lost their lives settling and defending the early untamed territory of "The Dark and Bloody Ground." Because of our directly traceable lineage to Francis and Peter Cossart as well to Henry Comingore, my siblings and I, our children and all their direct descendants may claim our true birthright – among the proudest of American Heritages, the title of Son or Daughter of the American Revolution.

CHAPTER TEN - THE ILLINOIS COSATS

My Great, Great Grandfather, David Cosat[10] as mentioned above was born October 10, 1812 in Harrodsburg, Mercer County, Kentucky. Note this is the final change in the spelling of my mother's paternal family name in her lineage from the original French "Cossart." Today there are literally dozens of variations on the Cossart name in America, and it is said the offspring of Peter Cossart account for the greatest number of variations of spelling of the surname of any branch of the family. David's father, Jacob, died in Mount Pleasant, Kentucky on September 11, 1822 when David was but 10 years of age.

The Reverend Jacob was laid to rest in the Kirby-Whitenack family graveyard on Mt. Pleasant Pike in Mercer County where his headstone still stands and remains readable. The photo of his headstone above is compliments of James Streeter of the "Dutch Cousins". David's mother Margaret Comingore, survived her husband by nearly twenty years, passing June 2, 1842 in Kentucky. As previously explained, many of their offspring would go on to settle new frontiers, aided by legislation passed to encourage expansion of the population into the Northwest Territories.

Once the Constitution had been adopted, Congress turned attention to other pressing matters. The boundaries of the Northwest Territories had been established by an Act of Congress in 1787. However, the British and French maintained an ongoing military and trading presence there, even long after the Revolution and the defeat of the Indian Alliance in 1794. The War of 1812 culminated with General Andrew Jackson's bloody defeat of the British at the Battle of New Orleans in January, 1815, a victory so one-sided it is not at all inaccurate to term it a slaughter. Though no new boundaries were actually drawn in the treaty ending the war, Jackson's convincing victory over the British at New Orleans greatly bolstered what had been, up to that point in time, America's somewhat tentative sense of independence and finally ended the lingering British hold on the Northwest Territory as well. A new era of confidence and optimism for the nation's future ensued.

Having finally rid themselves of the British in the Northwest, the US government needed a way to secure its claims to the land. But most of the soldiers who had fought in the Revolution and in the War of 1812 had returned to civilian life after the war. The standing American Army was far too small to occupy and protect the vast expanse of the Northwest Territories, and the fledgling nation was still heavily in debt from the costs of fighting two wars. Addressing both problems at once, a public lands sales act was adopted by Congress in 1820 making lands of the Northwest Territories available at very attractive prices for anyone who would come and homestead it. Furthermore, many land grants were made in the territories in payment for war debts and as rewards, so-called "bounty lands", for veterans of those wars. Much of the land around Vincennes and Terre Haute, Indiana was granted the early French settlers who were already long-established there. After all, France had been a vital and critically important ally to the colonies in the War for Independence.

Because of the rush for land in the territories after the War of 1812, a phenomenon that became known as "the Land Craze", the population of the Ohio, Indiana and Illinois Territories quickly swelled. Thanks to the population explosion and some "creative" census taking, in 1818 thirty-one years after the Northwest Territory boundaries had been drawn, Illinois achieved statehood. Indiana had achieved statehood two years earlier in 1816, having been settled largely by migrants from Kentucky. Settlers from Kentucky, Ohio and Indiana would also help feed the growth of Illinois. Seeing a bright future in store for the new state, on October 10, 1829 David Cossart's Uncle Albert purchased 80 acres in Vermilion County in Section W2SE, Township 20N, Range 12W for the price of $100.

Before the land craze, the Illinois Territory had been known for its abundant wild fur, and later in the early 1820's at Danville, for its saline springs, salt being more valuable than gold at the time. In fact, it was primarily fur and salt that originally drew trappers and settlers to the region. Later still, it became known for its rich coal deposits. However, as more and more settlers arrived during the land craze, the rich, deep soil of woodland and prairie was increasingly turned to the plow, and agriculture was to become the main industry of the state. About 1832 David Cosat with siblings, Peter, Henry, and Jacob Commingore Cosat followed their Uncle Albert's example and removed from Mercer County, Kentucky to Vermilion County, Illinois. They had come to lay claim to their own piece of that bright agricultural future.

"...nature's bounty vastly impressed people in frontier Illinois. The rich, deep soil was fertile - incredibly fertile to those from rocky New England and sandy stretches of northern Europe - and the growing season was long. In addition, the frontier teemed with game, enjoyed both sufficient precipitation and good drainage, and sported many navigable streams. Stands of fine timber graced Illinois, especially in southern Illinois and along waterways. Inexpensive land awaited ordinary people." [59]

The "ordinary people" of whom Davis speaks were not so ordinary by today's standards. To a man, these were proud, hard-working folk who were self-reliant out of necessity. As related by H.W. Beckwith in his opening address at the first meeting of the Vermilion County Old Settler's Association, held September, 1885, "Every man in those pioneer days was his own carpenter. He tinkered up his own wagon; made his mold-boards of wood for his plow; mended his harness; made his cradles and his bedsteads. He was a shoemaker, and had the implements, very few and crude, often implements of his own make, with which he made the shoes that his wife and children wore. The mothers or elder daughters took the wool as it came from the back of the sheep, carded it into rolls, spun it into yarn and wove it into fabrics. They broke the flax and made the tow and linen with which her under garments and lighter summer wear were composed. I have seen whole families in Danville clad in garments thus made at home.

People were rough in their exterior, in their polish, in their manner. Those were the days of physical manhood ; when a man was regarded as a man because he had physical strength, and so with the partner of his joys and his cares. She, too, was to be a person of great bodily strength, and of great courage, who would fight a wolf or an Indian at her door, as a bear would fight for her cubs." [20]

Thankfully, David and his siblings were not destined to experience the kind of bloody warfare for the land his parents and grandparents had known in Kentucky. By the time of their arrival in Illinois, though Indian tribes still resided in the area, resistance to the white man's advance had been virtually crushed. In the last uprising in Illinois of any consequence, the defeat of Sauk Chief Black Hawk in August, 1832 ended a 15-week war in which the Sauk tribe was almost annihilated. Soldiers and settlers killed numbered 70 - Indians killed: 492. Thereafter, though minor altercations with the remaining tribes still sometimes occurred, with their numbers, lands, and power rapidly dwindling, and the numbers of whites ever increasing, the truth could no longer be denied. The changes they had seen coming and had so mightily resisted for so long were by then a barreling freight train of unstoppable momentum.

By the mid to late 1830's the woodlands and prairies of the Wabash and Vermilion River Valleys, home for hundreds of years to the Oabache, the Miami, the Kickapoo and the Pottawatomie tribes lay unresisting, available for the taking of white settlers to come and build their farms and domesticate the land. A new age had dawned in the Northwest Territory, and it was clear the Red Man had to go. The struggle to decide who would retain dominion over the land was finished, and as always has been the case, to the victor belonged the spoils. The following from History of Vermilion County, H W Beckwith, 1879 [12], describes the sorrow-filled and undignified exodus of a once great and proud Potowatomie nation on what became infamously known as "The Trail of Death."

"The final migration of the Potowatomies from the Wabash Valley was under charge of Col. Pepper and Gen. Tipton and took place in the summer of 1838. It was a sad sight, these children of the forest being driven from the homes of their childhood. Bidding farewell to the hills, valleys and streams of their infancy, the graves of their revered ancestors, leaving these sacred scenes to be desecrated by the plowshares of the white man. No wonder the downcast warriors wept-the old men trembled and the swarthy cheek of the youth paled. There were about one thousand persons of all ages in the line of march.

Reluctantly they wended their way toward the setting sun, watching their chances to break into the brush and return to their dearly loved homes, saying they would rather die than leave their country. When they reached Danville they halted several days being in want of food. Without tents, and a liberal supply of food, there was much suffering among them. While at Danville they camped on the Dave Fowler farm. During their stay there were many deaths.

The mournful procession passed on across Illinois, without adequate means of conveyance for the weak, the aged and the infirm. Several years later the Miami Nation was removed to their western homes by coercive means under an escort of United States troops. This once proud and powerful nation was far inferior in point of numbers to the Pottowatomies. Their removal took the last of the original proprietors of the section, thenceforth to be known as Vermilion County, Illinois, to beyond the Mississippi river. This left the fields and plains, the woods and rivers, which had been the red man's home to the use of the white man."

With the Indian threat eliminated there was time for the luxury of pangs of conscience by some, especially those who had never lost friend or immediate family members to the tomahawk of the Red Man. It's certainly fair to say over the years there had been atrocities enough committed by both sides. The exodus of the vanquished tribes described by Beckwith had taken place less than a century, indeed within one human lifespan, of the time my mother was born in the Vermilion County Seat of Danville. I remember her speaking of the stories handed down by her parents and grandparents of the terrible mistreatment suffered by the Indians at the hands of the whites in those times. While certainly proud of her ancestral heritage, she also seemed to have a great deal of sympathy for the Native American, and later in her life she contributed to a number of charitable causes to benefit various Native American tribes.

Becoming part of the irresistible tide of white settlement, in August of 1835 David Cosat purchased at $1.25 per acre, 40 acres in Section 14 of Blount Township and an additional contiguous 40 acres in December that year. Having established his own homestead and laid a foundation for a future, on January 14, 1836 at Danville, David took Nancy Truax as his bride, born May 9, 1817 in Lexington, Kentucky, daughter of Benjamin Traux. The Benjamin Traux homestead, established in 1830, lay less than two miles northwest of David's 1835 purchase. Interestingly, in researching the Truax branch of the family I found they also were among the earliest European settlers to come to the New World, having arrived in the first group of colonists to New Amsterdam from Leyden, Holland aboard the ship "New Netherlands" in 1624. I find it remarkable so many of these early American families remained close neighbors through multiple migrations over periods of hundreds of years.

In 1837, the year following his marriage to Nancy Traux, two separate Federal land patents were issued David for his 80 acres. David apparently did well for himself on their farm. Illinois land records show on May 9, 1849 he acquired three additional parcels by Federal Warrant in the western and eastern portions of the township, bringing his total holdings to just under 235 acres.

As for the town of Danville, from fond memories of my own childhood when we visited my mother's home town in the 1950's, I remember it as a quiet, charming little town of shady tree-lined residential streets, tidy lawns and parks with well-kept floral gardens and placid lakes swimming with swans and ducks and geese. Apparently, it was not always so. So, what was it like a century and a quarter before when David Cosat arrived there? Henry Harbaugh was an early resident of Vermilion County, arriving in Danville from Cincinnati in 1836, the same year David Cosat was married there. Quoted in Beckwith's History of Vermilion County [12] Henry's recollection of the town at that time was anything but laudatory.

"Well, Danville was a poor town. It was the miserablest town I ever did see. I did not want to stay here. Why nobody wanted to stay here. There was nothing but hazel brush. Many of the cabins which had been built were abandoned, while those who owned them had gone to the edge of the timber to herd their stock and raise something to eat. Danville was most all hazel brush and deserted log cabins." Small wonder, I suppose, that David had chosen to settle in the fertile, well-timbered lands of neighboring Blount Township and away from the Danville of 1836.

There, northwest of Danville, David and Nancy cleared and worked the land, made their home and raised their family. Unfortunately, though the Indian threat had been subdued, raising a family in that time and place would prove to be much more difficult than either of them might have wished. As it had been for their forbears in Kentucky, the weather remained a formidable adversary for the early Illinois settler. The very first winter David and Nancy weathered in their little cabin brought a storm of historic proportion. December 20, 1836 dawned a mild balmy day in Illinois, welcome I'm sure, but unusual for that time of year. There was no way to know what the wrath of nature would bring them later that day. For many caught outside, away from shelter, it would prove fatal.

"Snow melt covered Illinois with pools and slush... a fast-moving front sliced eastward, freezing pools and slush solid in minutes. Persons caught in the open raced for shelter, many not making it. Cattle, hogs, birds and other animals froze fast to the ground and died. One quick-thinking horseman sliced open his horse and crawled inside it to stay warm; there he was found, frozen to death. Andrew Heredith, driving over 1000 hogs toward St. Louis, reached a point 8 miles south of Scottville when the cold front hit. He and his assistants fled by wagons to safety, barely making it, but anguished hogs piled upon each other for warmth. Those on the bottom suffocated, while those on the outside of the pile froze, creating a pyramid of 500 dead hogs. Surviving hogs suffered horribly."

"...For decades survivors reckoned dates of births, marriages, deaths and other important events from the Deep Snow, or the Sudden Freeze. Survivors prided themselves on having borne nature's fury, considering themselves true settlers - "the "Old Settlers" - and regarding later arrivals as untested upstarts." [59]

Bringing new life into the world on the backwoods frontier was highly risky too, both for mother and infant, especially when complications arose. Families had access to medical aid only very rarely, and daily life itself in the frontier of the 1800's was often unkind. Disease and accidents took their toll, and the long-term survival rate among children that did manage to survive the travails of the birth process was not high.

"Picture the horrors of isolation in times of emergency--wife or child suddenly taken desperately ill, and no physician within a hundred miles; husband or son hovering between life and death as the result of injury by a falling tree, a wild beast, a venomous snake, an accidental gun-shot, or the tomahawk of a prowling Indian. Who shall describe the anxiety, the agony, which in some measure must have been the lot of every frontier family? The prosaic illnesses of the flesh were troublesome enough. On account of defective protection for the feet in wet weather, almost everybody had rheumatism; most settlers in the bottom-lands fell victims to fever and ague [malaria] at one time or another; even in the hill country few persons wholly escaped malarial disorders. 'When this home-building and land-clearing is accomplished,' wrote one whose recollections of the frontier were vivid, 'a faithful picture would reveal not only the changes that have been wrought, but a host of prematurely brokedown men and women, besides an undue proportion resting peacefully in country graveyards.'" [38]

The first child of David and Nancy's union, a daughter, died the same day she was born on November 2, 1836 and the second, a son, born December 5, 1837 shared the same fate. Neither child lived long enough to be named. In fact, it was customary in those times not to name a child until it seemed likely they would actually survive. Perhaps it was an emotional defense of sorts, for it was not at all uncommon to lose newborn children. David and Nancy's first child to live beyond her day of birth on February 17, 1839, Maria Ann, died at the age of 10. Another, Susan Jane, born March, 1846, died just days shy of her third birthday in 1849. Yet another, Elizabeth Ellen, born 18 March, 1848, died the 31st of March the following year, barely having passed her first birthday.

The close proximity of the dates of death of Maria, Susan and Elizabeth in March of 1849 suggests they may well have died from a common cause, perhaps some communicable disease that was wreaking havoc in the family. Death records were not required in that day, and no comprehensive public health records were kept. However, we find 1849 was a year in which a great cholera epidemic swept the state of Illinois, and indeed, devastated the population across much of the nation. It seems very likely these three young Cosats were unfortunate victims of that great epidemic.

The cholera strain prevalent that year in the West was said to be a particularly virulent one. Dr. William McPheeters, who treated cholera patients during the 1849 outbreak in St. Louis described its symptoms thusly. "vomiting freely with frequent and copious discharges from the bowels; at first of slight bilious character, but it soon became pure 'rice water'; cramps in the stomach and lower extremities and tongue cold; skin of a blue color and very much corrugated; urinary secretions suspended; eyes sunken and surrounded by a livid hue."[64] It would not have been an easy or pretty death, but for those who did succumb, it was invariably swift.

Professor Turner of Illinois College in a letter to a friend describes the swift lethality of the disease in the first great outbreak of cholera in Illinois in 1833. "From this time the daily yea, the hourly report, was 'He is sick,' 'He is dead,' 'He is buried.' To meet a man at night and attend his funeral in the morning has ceased to alarm, much less to surprise. Some die in three hours, seldom do they live twelve, and very rarely twenty-four. As I have walked through the streets in the evening, I have seen through the windows and doors the sick and the dying, sometimes four or five in the same room in a log hut, some on the bed, others on the floor, and perhaps one or two sorrow-smitten beings crawling from bed to bed to give a cup of water or to brush away the flies. On every face was written 'Woe,' and on every doorpost 'Death,' and on not a few 'Utter desolation.'...For some weeks not a soul was seen approaching from the country, except here and there a man on a horse upon the full run for The doctor! The doctor! For Heaven's sake, sir, can't you tell me where is the doctor? My father is dying, my wife is dead, and my children are dying.' ..."[64]

The fact is, in the case of cholera it was probably a good thing for those on the rural frontier that they had no access to a physician in those times. Given the lack of medical understanding of pathogen-borne disease often the "cures" were as terrible as the illness and though well-intended, practically amounted to torture of the victim. Cholera treatments routinely included heavy bleeding of the patient by lancing a vein in the arm, massive oral doses of calomel, a chalky mercury compound, "until the gums begin to bleed", rubbing of the body with mustard, turpentine, and cayenne pepper, sulphuric ether, large enemas of "chicken tea" and salt, tobacco smoke enemas, plugging of the rectum with beeswax and oilcloth, electric shock therapy, and on, and on. If the patient by chance did recover, it was only in spite of the treatment, certainly not because of it. Those who did survive were often left with lifelong disabilities resulting from the treatments themselves. Times of serious illness in the mid-19th Century were desperate times indeed.

It may have been the 1849 cholera outbreak and loss of three of his children within the course of a few weeks that caused David to sell off his land and strike out for Wisconsin to join his father-in-law there. With the discovery of lead deposits in Wisconsin, Benjamin Truax had gone there with an aim to making a fortune in mining. Apparently, David Cosat found no fortune there, for a year later he returned to Blount Township and purchased 120 acres from B. M. Kirk at $5 per acre. He returned to what he knew best - farming, raising crops, cattle and horses.

The twelfth and last child to be borne by Nancy Truax Cosat was Sarah Helen, born May 1, 1858. Nancy died on May 8th, one week after giving birth to Sarah, and one day short of her 41st birthday. I don't know for certain, but the timing suggests she may have died of complications of a difficult birth. Infant Sarah survived only a little longer than her mother, passing on May 20th. With no mother to suckle her or a wet nurse to serve as surrogate, chances of the frontier infant's survival were almost nil. One can only imagine the grief and despair David must have felt, having lost both the child and his wife and life's partner within the space of two weeks.

After an appropriate mourning period, David remarried on January 15, 1860 to Sarah A Cox, born 1808 in Kentucky. With Sarah at age 52 and already beyond normal child-bearing years, there were no children by his second marriage. But the reality of those times required two to make a home and raise a family. A man with children and a farm needed a wife to tend to domestic duties, while he worked the land and made a living for the family. I have no way of knowing of course, but I would guess the marriage to Sarah may have been a marriage of convenience for both of them, as was common practice for the times.

By all measures of the age, David Cosat, an honest, law-abiding, hard-working citizen of the new nation and the even newer state of Illinois, had provided well for his family, acquiring considerable lands, while contributing to the advance of white civilization and domestication of the new frontier. Surpassing his allotted three-score-and-ten, at the age of 73 on February 26, 1886 in Danville David passed into history and went to his final rest. His remains lie in Blount Township in Fairchild Cemetery in the Illinois Nature Preserve northwest of Danville. The burial ground is situated near the original property line between David's Father-in-Law, Benjamin Truax's homestead and the neighboring Fairchild family homestead.

As was more or less typical of the times, of David and Nancy's children, only half survived to adulthood. Thankfully for me and mine, one of the six survivors was my Great Grandfather, John James Cosat[11], born March 31, 1844, the sixth of David and Nancy's twelve. The other five of his siblings who survived to adulthood were John Benjamin Cosat, born 7 August, 1840, Mary Margaret Cosat, born 16 March, 1842, Rachael Cosat, born 5 May, 1850, David Cosat, Jr., born 27 October, 1852, and Nancy Emmaline Cosat, born 27 May, 1854. [See the family photo in Appendix V.]

John James led an illustrious life in his own right. A highly principled abolitionist, at the age of 20 while in Wisconsin, he enlisted in the Union Army with the rank of Corporal, joining Company I of the 5th Wisconsin Volunteer Infantry. The following is from Past and Present of Vermilion County, Illinois, 1903 [31], by C. G. Pearson and S.J. Clarke. "At the time of the Civil War he was an earnest advocate of the Union Cause and on the 14th of July 1864, he enlisted in Company I, 5th Wisconsin Volunteers, under Captain Thomas Flint and Colonel E. A. Allen, joining the army at Broadhead, Wis." While his unit remained in Wisconsin, John James married Miss Frances H Rosebaum on September 11, 1864. Shortly thereafter on September 21 the 5th Wisconsin was ordered to the front, and on

Oct 2nd they left the state. John James' new bride was already pregnant with their first child.

The bio of John James continues, "In the fall of 1864 the regiment was transferred to the Army of the Potomac and operated with that Great military division until 1865. Mr. Cosat participated in the Battle of Petersburg and in the sanguinary engagement at Sailors Run. Because of meritorious conduct and marked bravery he was recommended by General Grant for a Commission. With his command he pursued General Lee to Appomattox."

The official War Record of the Appomattox Campaign [6] details the exemplary bravery that led to John James' recommendation for a Commission. "On April 5, A.D. 1865, in the battle of Sailor's Run, Virginia, Sergeant Augus Cameron, Corporal Charles Roughan, Corporal August Becker, and Private Jown W. Davis of Company "C" and Corporal John J. Cosat and Private Heron W. True of Company "I", all of the 5th Wisconsin Volunteer Infantry, captured and took prisoner Lieutenant General Ewell, staff and body-guard and through them his entire command, consisting of 6,000 officers and men, 10 pieces of artillery, 100 wagons; 600 horses and mules and their equipment and 6,000 stands of small arms and for which received the compliments of both Generals Grant and Meade and a promise of recommendation for promotion."

So how in the world did six lone Union soldiers accomplish such an amazing feat? The following description of the event is from The Disciples of Christ in Illinois, by Nathaniel S. Haynes, 1915 [35].

"On the morning of Apr. 6, 1865, Lieutenant-General Ewell had placed his corps on the brow of a hill south of Sailor's Creek. This Confederate force was savagely and simultaneously assaulted by the Second and Sixth Federal Corps, and with such skill and determination as to virtually destroy it. In this assault,

Mr. Cosat and five of his comrades were separated from their regiment, with the Confederate forces between them. The official war report of Thomas S Allen, colonel in command of the regiment, War Records, History of the Appomattox Campaign, page 953, gives the names of the six men, to wit: 'Sergeant Augus Cameron, Corporal Charles Roughan, Corporal August Becker, and Private Jown W. Davis of Company "C" and Corporal John J. Cosat and Private Heron W. True of Company "I", all of the 5th Wisconsin Volunteer Infantry'.

Sergeant Cameron suggested that they try to capture General Ewell. The six men ran across an open field and took position in a fence row that had grown up in dense brush. The sergeant crawled to the end of this, and reported that General Ewell, his staff and body-guard, probably a hundred in all, were riding directly toward them. The sergeant ordered that, when the Confederates came within hearing distance, they move in single file with cocked guns out of the brush-the sixth man stopping at the edge - and he himself would demand the surrender. General Ewell, thus completely surprised and supposing there were many Federals concealed in the brush, at once ordered his adjutant-general (Beglar) to unfurl the white flag, which he did. Shortly thereafter this immortal six had the honor of presenting to General Meade this famous old, battle scarred veteran of the Confederacy, his staff and body-guard, as prisoners of war!"

The following excerpt from Chapter XX of History of Green County Wisconsin, Union Publishing Co, 1884 [17], gives a little more detail about the fighting that took place at Sailor's Creek. "On the afternoon of April 3, they joined in the pursuit of Lee – the 6th corps encountering Gen. Ewell's forces at Little Sailor's Creek on the 7th. The lines were hurriedly formed and pushed forward at double-quick; the regiment marching with unbroken line through a swamp waist-deep, under fire of the enemy's musketry. They moved to the brow of a hill, where the enemy was discovered but a few paces distant, admirably posted, and fighting with the energy of despair. The regiment was in an extremely hazardous position, being subjected to a severe flank and cross fire. Col. Allen rode in advance of the line as calmly as though danger were unknown. Company G, (Capt. Henry Curran) and company C, (Lieut. Evan R. Jones) were deployed as skirmishers. Lieut.-Gen. Ewell and staff surrendered to six men of the skirmishers, under command of Sergt. Cameron, company A, who was promoted lieutenant on the field for gallantry. The action of the regiment elicited high encomiums from the corps, division and brigade commanders. In the action of April 7, the regiment had sixteen killed, seventy-nine wounded, and three died of wounds. The pursuit was continued until the 9th, when Lee surrendered."

The 5th Wisconsin mustered out June 20, 1865 in Madison, Wisconsin, counting 329 fatalities within the ranks. John certainly must have seen his share of bloodshed and death during his service. The War Between the States was the bloodiest ever waged on American soil. In the slaughter at Sailor's Creek alone, total casualties numbered nearly 10,000 men, most of whom were Confederate soldiers.

According to Disciples of Christ in Illinois, John James became a school teacher after returning to civilian life. However, he is also indicated a farmer by occupation in several subsequent population censuses. In 1871 Elder Cosat became the "Reverend" Cosat when he was ordained a Minister of the Gospel. He served as Justice of the Peace and a Pastor in the Old Union Church northwest of Danville. Census records show he also served as an enumerator for Blount Township in the 1880 Mortality Census. Interestingly, of the 26 who died in the county for the period covered by the census, June 1, 1879 through May 31, 1880, more than half (fourteen) were under the age of 20, and twenty of the twenty-six were less than 60 years of age. It seems in that age for a man to live out his allotted "three-score--and-ten" was the exception, rather than the rule.

Though tragic for John James and Dora, it was fortunate for me and mine, I suppose, John's first wife, Francis Rosebaum, died young in February, 1868. On July 11, 1869 John James Cosat remarried to young Miss Emma Cline, born September 11, 1851. Emma was the daughter of Nathaniel Cline of Blount Township, Vermilion County. Emma, being only seventeen at the time had to have her widowed mother, Cynthia, sign for her marriage license. Emma's father, a gunsmith to the Indians and an Illinois pioneer land owner, had died in 1863 in Gallatin, Tennessee. While serving as a fifer in the Union Army, he became a casualty of the war. Between 1870 and 1895 Emma bore John 12 children, one of whom was my Grandfather, Francis Marion Cosat[12], born February 19, 1889.

According to family Bible records, Francis' siblings, my Great Uncles and Aunts, in order of birth were Earnest Hannibal, born May 15, 1870, Pleasant, born May 5, 1872, Theodore Warren, born September 3, 1873, John David, born October 25, 1875, Lafayette, born August 26, 1877, Everett Monroe, born September 25, 1878, Effie Lewkethie Candice, born April 23, 1881, Charles Leroy, born December 23, 1883, Nellie Blanche, born September 12, 1886/7, Homer Raymond, born May 5, 1892 and Russell Lowell, born June 30, 1894. According to the same record, both Homer and Lowell died in infancy. However, the 1900 Census indicates Lowell was still living at age 4 and had been born in June 1895, not 1894.

Government documents reveal on July 10, 1890 John James Cosat applied for his Civil War veteran's pension. He was fortunate to draw that hard-earned pension for quite some time afterward, passing twenty-eight years later, on September 3, 1918 at the age of 74. Ten months prior to his death, at the time of his admission to the Old Soldier's Home, he was afflicted with arteriosclerosis, cardiac hypertrophy, prostate hypertrophy and chronic rheumatism. Per Home records, John suffered a Cerebral Hemorrhage and died in the hospital. The value of his personal effects at the time of his death was appraised at ten cents. What a pity it seems a man of his caliber should have died a near penniless pauper, but his purpose in life obviously was not to amass a fortune, rather to serve his fellow man and his God. John James Cosat had done so very well. According to the same home record, his remains were "returned to Danville Ill for burial." His grave, #224, lies with 436 others in the Circle of Civil War Soldiers, Springhill Cemetery, where the monument below had been dedicated to the county's Civil War Veterans in 1900.

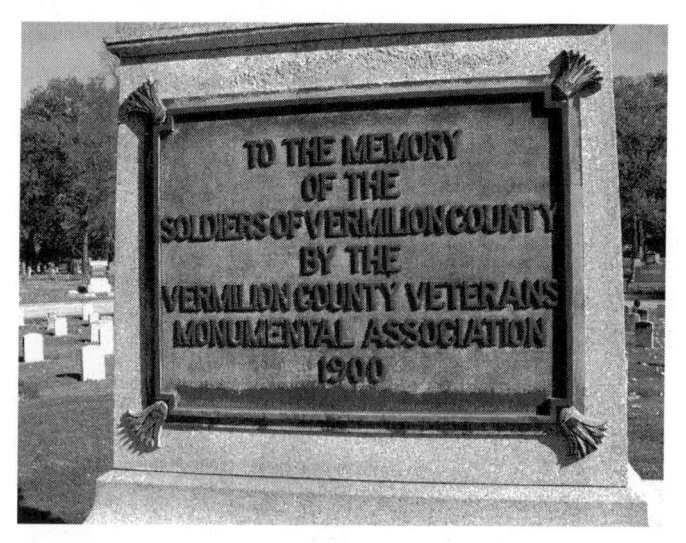

On October 5th in the year of his death, John's surviving widow, Emma Cline Cosat, applied for benefits on John's Civil War pension. She lived the remainder of her life in Danville with their son, Theodore Warren Cosat. Fifteen years after John James' death, on December 11, 1933 my Great Grandma Emma Cline Cosat passed away, at last joining her husband in the fullness of her years at age 82.

Soldier's Circle Monument, Springhill Cemetery, Danville Illinois

CHAPTER ELEVEN - TWENTIETH CENTURY CHANGES

Regrettably, I have virtually no information on my Grandfather Francis' early years, but at the age of 28 in 1917, Francis Marion Cosat registered for the World War One draft. According to his draft card, he had been married prior to the time of registration, but he was separated from his wife. Residing at 1013 Chandler Street in Danville, he told the interviewer he was unsure at the time whether he was divorced or not. The record also indicates he had previously served three years as a Private in the Artillery in the Illinois National Guard. He was employed at the time of his registration by Southern Printing Company of Little Rock, Arkansas.

Grandpa Francis' first marriage at some point was apparently terminated in divorce. I have not learned his first wife's name, the circumstances of the divorce, or whether there had been children by the marriage. However, subsequent to his divorce he remarried to my Grandmother Yeteva (Eva) Corder of Spencer, Indiana on March 18, 1920 at Lincoln Parsonage in Danville. The ceremony was presided over by Reverend J.D. Strouse and witnessed by Mrs. Emma Strouse, the pastor's wife.

At the time of their marriage, Francis was employed as a pressman at a local print shop in Danville, though he may have farmed as well. The photos below appear to have been taken behind a farm house in mid-summer of 1921, though I don't know specifically where the house was located. Eva is holding my mother, Dorothy June Cosat[13], their first child, born at 6:45 PM on June 7, 1921. The address of her birth was 309 Fairchild Street in Danville, which could well-be the address of the house in the photos. Interestingly, the attending physician was one Edward J Wheatley, MD. In the photo below, clenching a corncob pipe between his teeth, Grandpa, an avid fisherman, is rigging his fishing pole, perhaps preparing to go catch a bucket of catfish for supper.

Eva Cosat w/Dorothy, Danville, Illinois

Francis M Cosat Danville, Illinois

Siblings to follow Dorothy in order of birth were Mary Alice, Betty Jean, Robert Marion, Glen Edward, and William Eugene. By the 1930 census all of the six children of Francis and Eva Corder Cosat were born and living in Danville. As with most other American families, the Great Depression of the Thirties brought very hard economic times for the Cosats, and Grandpa had to travel far and wide looking for day work wherever it could be found. I still have cards and letters my mother saved, written in the Thirties by her father to the family back home in Danville while he was away, earning the "daily bread" in Fowler and Indianapolis, Indiana.

Sometime between 1937 and 1939 Eva moved to Indianapolis with the children. Although the move apparently had been initiated by my Grandmother due to marital problems, it appears the couple may have later reunited for a time. Francis' World War II draft card documents his address as of April 27, 1942 was 34 East Raymond Street in Indianapolis. Listed as a contact person on his draft card, my mother, "Mrs. Dorothy Wheatley" was living at 1101 West Congress Avenue. Francis' employer at the time was Joseph P. Rolles at 385 Century Building in Indianapolis. An employment certificate for Francis' sixteen year old son, Robert, indicates they were living at the East Raymond Street address as of November, 1942. Based on other documents my mother had kept among family memorabilia, by September of 1944 Francis and Eva had moved to 3716 E New York Street. At the time Grandma Eva was working outside the home, as were so many other women in the World War II era. It appears Grandpa remained in Indianapolis at least through the war years, based on a church newsletter and other family documents my mother kept.

The church newsletter, addressed to Francis M Cosat, 3716 East New York Street, dated February 28, 1945 was from the Olive Branch Christian Church. The subscription price, listed on the newsletter as 25 cents per year, gives one an idea of the austerity of the times. It contained an announcement relevant to the Cosat family. By this time Francis and Eva's son, my Uncle Robert Marion Cosat, was serving in the war as an Army paratrooper.

The clipping announced he had been wounded in Belgium in the Battle of the Bulge and had been awarded the Purple Heart. How poetic it seems, this ninth generation descendant of Jacques Cossart[4] had unwittingly returned after hundreds of years to the very place his ancestral family had first sought refuge from murder and oppression in France. There, more than four centuries later he very nearly laid down his own life, fighting to free that land, as well as France and the rest of Europe from the oppression of the brutal and bloodthirsty regime of the infamous Nazi dictator and mass murderer, Adolf Hitler.

Further documents help determine the chain of events and places of residence for the family through the Forties. Receipts for life insurance premiums paid by the youngest of the Cosat children, my Uncle William Eugene Cosat, dated September, 1944 and

March, 1946 indicate his residence of record was still at the New York Street address, although correspondence from him shows by 1946 he was in the Navy, serving at Pearl Harbor, Hawaii. My mother and father apparently were residing at the East New York Street address when I was born in 1946.

At some point, Grandma and Grandpa once again separated. Francis moved back to Danville, Illinois, where he had obtained a job working his trade as pressman in a print shop. There had been sea-change in society from the times when whole families for better or worse, stayed together their entire lives on the homestead, and family elders passed the land down to their children. More and more migrated to the cities to engage in business and all manner of commerce, and women had gained new independence. Though they never divorced, strained relations between my mother's parents ultimately led them to part ways forever. Grandma Eva Corder Cosat remained in Indianapolis, where she continued working a good job in the RCA factory on a vacuum tube assembly line. By my own recollection, by mid to late 1947 my mother, father, sister and I were living in Army family housing on Pleasant Run Boulevard in Indianapolis. The other Cosat children were all grown and gone from the family nest as well.

In December of 1948, Grandpa attended a fateful Christmas party in his employer's home in Danville. As the party was breaking up, the boss's daughter's car became stuck in a snowdrift in the street. While helping get the car unstuck, Grandpa slipped and fell underneath. Unaware, the driver backed up, and one of the rear wheels ran over his mid-section, breaking his pelvis and causing other internal injuries. Apparently, there was some difficulty in getting compensation to pay the hospital bills. Letters from my mother to her father during his hospitalization speak of getting an attorney to recover medical costs from his employer. Grandpa underwent two surgeries and months of painful convalescence. He appeared to be recovering, but to the family's shock and great dismay, on July 24, 1949 he died suddenly from complications of his injuries. Three days later Francis Marion Cosat was laid to rest in Johnson Cemetery northwest of Danville, within a few miles of the original Cosat homestead where his grandfather, David, had settled in 1835.

The faded, somewhat grainy old photo above was taken in Danville at the home of grandpa's sister-in-law, my Great Aunt

Lillian Corder-Martin, shortly before his death. Grandpa is standing with his cane next to my mother. My older sister, Phyllis, I, and our father are seated on the garden bench. As of this writing, of the happy, beaming faces in this photo, I am sole survivor. As I recall, I had been playing "cowboys and Indians" in the yard when the family gathered for the photo. Aunt Lillian was the family historian in those days, and she or her husband, Les Martin, took this shot with Lillian's always-present Kodak Brownie camera. At the time it was taken I was not pleased with being rounded up long enough to sit for it; hence, the frown on my face. Today, I am very thankful to have it, as it is reminiscent of a simpler, happy time and is a reminder of the grandpa I never really had the chance to know. It was the last photo taken of him before he died.

Now, a lifetime later, they all have since passed one-by-one beyond the veil into eternity. I am happy to assume the mantle of keeper of the story of our family for a while, until it is finally my time to join them on the other side. It is my hope this book will serve as a vehicle to pass that story on to generations to follow, that they who paved the way for us may continue to live in the hearts and minds of their descendants.

"A man is never truly gone until forgotten..."

APPENDIX I - CHARLEMAGNE LINEAGE

Below is the ancestral lineage from Louis duBois, Great Grandfather of Margaret Van Nest Cossart, going back to Charlemagne the Great. The source for Generation 1 is "Register of Qualified Huguenot Ancestors of the National Huguenot Society" (Bloomington, MN 1995), page 74. Generations 2 thru 32 were provided by the Registrar General, Order of the Crown of Charlemagne in the United States of America

1. LOUIS DUBOIS, baptized at Lillie, France on 13 Nov 1626; died at Kingston, NY on 23 Jun 1693; married at French Church Mannheim on 10 Oct 1655 to CATHERINE BLANCHAN, daughter of Matthew Blanchan. Left Mannheim for America circa 1660, settled at New Paltz, NY.

2. Louis DuBois was the child of CHRETIEN DUBOIS who was born at Tournai, Flanders in 1597; died at Flanders about 1628; married about 1621 to CORNELIA BRUNEL who was born at Tournai about 1599 and died at Province of Flanders.

3. Chretian DuBois was the child of JEAN DUBOIS who was born at Vermille, Flanders in 1566.

4. Jean DuBois was the child of CHARLES DUBOIS DEFIENNS who died in 1607; married about 1558, BARBE DEBEAUFREMEZ who died in 1580.

5. Charles DuBois Defienns was the child of ANTOINE DUBOIS DE FIENNES who married BAUDOUINE LIONNEL.

6. Antoine DuBois Defiennes was the child of CLAUDINE DE LANNOY who was born about 1507; married to CLAUDE DU BOIS DE FIENNES who was born about 1482; died after his will was made 3 Apr 1548.

7. Claudine De Lannoy was the child of JEAN IV DE LANNOY, SR. MAINGOVAL who married second PHILIPPINE DE PLAINES.

8. Jean IV De Lannoy, Sr. Maingoval was the child of JEAN III DE LANNOY who died at Cannes de Valenciennes in 1498; married first CATHERINE DE NEUVILLE.

9. Jean III De Lannoy was the child of ANTOINE DE LANNOY, SR. MAINGOVAL who married in 1419, MARIE DE VILLE.

10. Antoine De Lannoy, Sr. Maingoval was the child of JEAN I DE LANNOY who married JEAN DE CROY.

11. Jean I De Lannoy was the child of HUGHES II DE LANNOY who died at Lys, France after 1373; married MARIE BERLAIMONT.

12. Hughes II De Lannoy was the child of HUGHES DE LANNOY who was born about 1311; died at Lys, France in Jun 1349; married in 1329, MARGUERITE, DAME DE MAINGOVAL who died at Lys, France.

13. Marguerite, Dame of Maingoval was the child of JEAN DE FRANCHIMONT who was born about 1280; married about 1310, MAHIENNE DE LANNOY who was born about 1290.

14. Jean De Franchimont was the child of HELLIN II DE FRANCHIMONT who was married to AGNES (AGNIS) DE DURAS.

15. Hellin II De Franchimont was the child of AGNES OF BAVARIA who was born after 1229; married to HELLIN DE FRANCHIMONT who was born about 1245.

16. Agnes of Bavaria was the child of AGNES OF BRUNSWICK who was born after 1229; married OTTO II, DUKE OF BAVARIA.

17. Agnes of Brunswick was the child of HENRY IV, DUKE OF BRUNSWICK who was born in 1174; died in 1227; married in 1193, AGNES DU RHIN who was born in 1177.

18. Henry IV, Duke of Brunswick was the child of MATILDA OF ENGLAND who was born in London in 1156; died in Brunswick on 28 Jun 1189; buried at Church of St. Blaise (Blasius), now Brunswick Cathedral, Brunswick, Germany; married at Minden on 1 Feb 1168, HENRY "THE LION," DUKE OF SAXONY who was born in 1129; died at Brunswick on 6 Aug 1195; buried at Church of St. Blaise, Brunswick.

19. Matilda of England was the child of HENRY II, KING OF ENGLAND who was born at Le Mans on 5 Mar 1133; died at Chinon, Normandy on 6 Jul 1189; buried at Fontevrault Abbey, Anjou; married at Bordeaux on 18 May 1152, ELEANOR, DUCHESS OF AQUITAINE who was born at Bordeaux/Belin on 1122; died at Mirabell Castle, Poitiers on 31 Mar/Apr 1204; buried at Fontevrault Abbey, Anjou.

20. Henry II, King of England was the child of MATILDA OF ENGLAND, widow of Henry V, Emperor of Germany who was born at Winchester Castle, Hants, or London on 7 Feb 1102; died at Rouen, Normandy on 10 Sep 1167; buried at Bec Abbey; married at Le Mans, Maine on 22 May 1127, GEOFFREY (PLANTAGENET) V, COUNT OF ANJOU who was born on 24 Aug 1113; died at Chateau-du-Loire on 7 Sep 1151; buried at St. Julien's (now Le Mans Cathedral), Le Mans, Maine.

21. Matilda of England was the child of HENRY I, KING OF ENGLAND who was born at Selby, Yorks in the Autumn of 1068; died at Angers, Maine on 1 Dec 1135; buried at Reading Abbey, Berks; married at Westminster Abbey on 11 Nov 1100, (EDITH) MATILDA OF SCOTLAND who was born at Dunfermline in 1079; died at Westminster Palace on 1 May 1118.

22. Henry I, King of England was the child of MATILDA OF FLANDERS who was born about 1031; died at Caen on 2 Nov 1083; buried in the Church of the Holy Trinity, Caen; married at Eu about 1051, WILLIAM THE CONQUEROR, DUKE OF NORMANDY, KING OF ENGLAND who was born at Falaise, Normandy in the Autumn of 1028; died at Priory of St. Gervais, near Rouen on 9 Sep 1087; buried in the Abbey of St. Stephen, Caen.

23. Matilda of Flanders was the child of ADELE (ALIX) OF FRANCE who died on 8 Jan 1078/79; married in 1028, BALDWIN V DE LILLE, COUNT OF FLANDERS.

24. Adele (Alix) of France was the child of ROBERT II "THE PIOUS," KING OF FRANCE who was born at Orleans on 27 Mar 972; died at Meulan on 20 Jul 1031; buried in St. Denis; married the third time in 998, CONSTANCE OF ARLES, TOULOUSE & PROVENCE who was born in 986; died at Meulan on 25 Jul 1032.

25. Robert II, "The Pious," King of France was the child of HUGH CAPET (HUGUE CAPET), KING OF FRANCE was born about 940; died at Les Juifs, near Chartres; buried in St. Denis on 24 Oct 996; married about 970, ADELAIDE OF POITOU who was born about 950/955; died on 15 Jun 1004.

26. Hugh Capet (Hugue Capet), King of France was the child of HUGH MAGNUS (HUGUE THE GREAT) was born about 895; died at Dourdan; buried in St. Denis on 16 Jun 956; married the third time at Mainz before 14 Sep 937, HEDWIG OF SAXONY who was born about 922; died on 9 Jan 958 or 10 May 965.

27. Hugh Magnus (Hugue The Great), King of France was the child of BEATRIX OF VERMANDOIS who was born about 880; died after Mar 931; married about 890/95, ROBERT I, COUNT OF PARIS, KING OF FRANCE who was born in 866; died in a battle near Soissons on 15 Jun 923.

28. Beatrix of Vermandois was the child of HERBERT I, COMTE DE VERMANDOIS who was born about 850; died about 900/907; married probably LIEGARDUS.

29. Herbert I, Comte de Vermandois was the child of PIPPIN (PEPIN), COUNT OF SENLIS, PERONNE, AND ST. QUENTIN who was born about 815; died after 840

30. Pippin (Pepin), Count of Senlis, Peronne, and St. Quentin was the child of BERNARD, KING OF ITALY AND LOMBARDY was born in 797; died at Milan on 17 Apr 818; buried in St. Ambroisius, Milan; married about 814, CUNIGUNDE who died about 15 Jun 835.

31. Bernard, King of Italy was the child of PIPPIN (PEPIN, KARLMANN) KING OF ITALY who was born in 777; baptized in Rome on 15 Apr 781; died on 8 Jul 810; married probably a daughter of his Great Uncle, Duke Bernard.

32. Pepin, King of Italy was the child of CHARLEMAGNE, THE EMPEROR who was born at Ingelheim, Germany on 2 Apr 742; died at Aix-la-Chapelle (Aachen), Germany on 28 Jan 813/14; married at Aix-la-Chapelle (Aachen) about 771, HILDEGARDE OF SWABIA, COUNTESS OF VINZGUA (LINZGAU) who was born in 758; died 30 Apr 783; buried at Metz.

APPENDIX II

Below is a transcript of the October 12, 1662 Dutch West India Company record of purchase of passage on the Purmerlander Kerk by Jacques Cossart of Leiden, Holland. The ship's Captain is Benjamin Barentz.

```
"JACQUES COSSARIS"  debet--Voor vrocht en costght
day hy A° 1662, 12 October pr.'t Schip de Pumerlander Kerch
Schippr.  Benjamin Barentsen, is herewaerts
gecomen................................Fl.  39
Voor syn vrou.........................       39
En 1 kinder unter 10 jaren............      19½
                              T. Fl        97½
```

The Cossart surname has been Romanized to "Cossaris" in this record, a common practice by the Dutch in those times. Fare totaling 97 1/2 Florins is tabulated for Jacques, his wife, Lea Villeman, and one child, under age ten, Lea Cossart I. There was no charge for Suzanna, who was but 18 months old at the time of their Atlantic crossing. Complete passenger list is below:

Claes Paulusz, from Ditmarsen, and wife.
Nicholaes Du Pui, from Artois, wife and three children, 6, 5 and 2 yrs.
Ernou Du Tois, from Ryssel (Lisle), wife and child, 14 yrs. old.
Gideon Merlitt, wife and four children, 15, 8, 6, and 4 yrs.
Louis Lackman, wife and three children, 6, 4 and 2 yrs.
Jacques Cossaris, wife and two children, 5 and 1- 1/2 yrs. Old
Jan De Conchilier (Consilyea)
Jan Bocholte (Boeckholt), wife and five children, 13, 9, 8, 4 and 1 yr. old
Jacob Colff, from Leiden, wife and two children, 5 and 3 yrs.
Judith Jansz, maiden, from Leiden
Carsten Jansen
Ferdinandus De Mulder

Isaac Verniele, wife and four children, all over 20 yrs. of age.
Abelis Setskoorn
Claes Jansen Van Heyningen

APPENDIX III

Below is a scan of the Peter Cossart September, 1780 Land Book Warrant Entry for Lincoln County, Book 1, Page 83, Entry 25.

"Peter Cosseart assee ye enters 600 acres upon a Treasury Warrant on the head of the first Branch of muddy creek from the mouth as you go up on the right hand side of the Creek to include a Dry Spring and Some Saplins cut down"

Failing to raise a crop on the claim, the Cossart family later lost to other claims the 600 acres of virgin land Peter had reserved in the above recorded Treasury Warrant.

APPENDIX IV

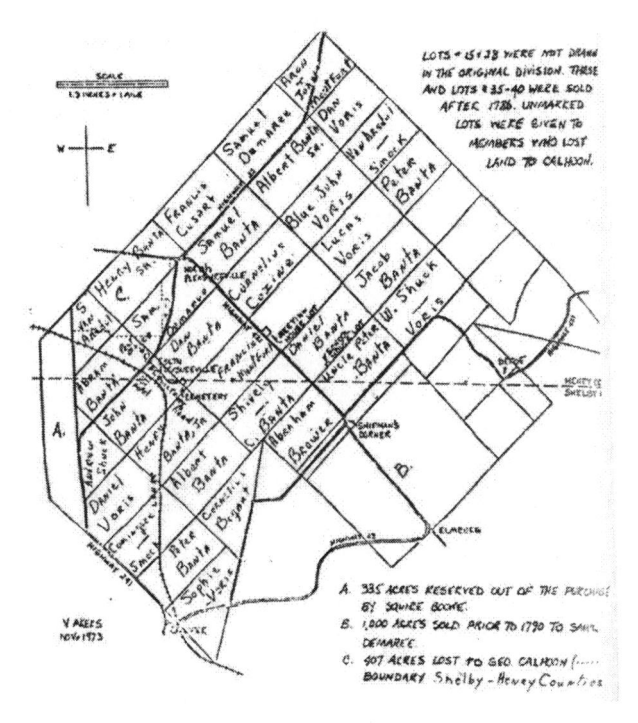

This 1973 drawing by Vincent Akers shows the layout of the Kentucky Low Dutch Tract, purchased from Squire Boone and eventually settled by about half of the survivors of the Dutch Conewago migrants. The tract lays astride the Henry and Shelby County line. The parcel purchased by Francis Cossart (Lot # 18) lay on the Northwest edge of the tract, between the parcels of Henry Banta and Samuel Demaree. The principal town of North Pleasureville is located just to the South of Cossart's lot, which is bounded on the Southeast by present-day Highway 22. The "Six-Mile Meeting House" which served as the Low Dutch church was located at the center of the community.

"As the word "Dutch" would suggest, Low Dutch who built the

Six Mile Meetinghouse were descendants of Holland Dutch, but with a good many French Huguenots mixed in. Their ancestors were some of the earliest European settlers in America, having immigrated to New Amsterdam during the decades before the English took over and renamed it New York in 1664.

They spent the next two centuries running away from the English, trying to avoid being sucked into the great American melting pot. They had a dream of a Dutch colony somewhere on the frontier with enough land to sustain generations of large families. Here they could preserve their language, church, customs and ethnic identity. With that dream, they rode the crest of the great wave of pioneers moving the American frontier ever westward. "

Vincent Akers

APPENDIX V

Above is a Cosat family portrait of my Great-Great Grandfather, David with his six surviving children. The photo was probably taken ca. 1882, a few years before David's death. David is seated with two of his daughters. Mary Margaret is to his left (I'm guessing, based on apparent relative ages) and Rachael, to his right. The youngest daughter, Nancy Emmaline, is standing immediately behind David. My Great Grandfather, John James, is standing at Emma's right, far left in the photo. He would have been about 38 when this photo was taken. The remaining two sons are John Benjamin, to Emmline's immediate left, and the youngest son at far right in the photo, David Cosat, Jr., born 1852. This photo, a treasured find for me, was shared on the Ancestry.com web site by a descendant of Emmaline.

APPENDIX VI

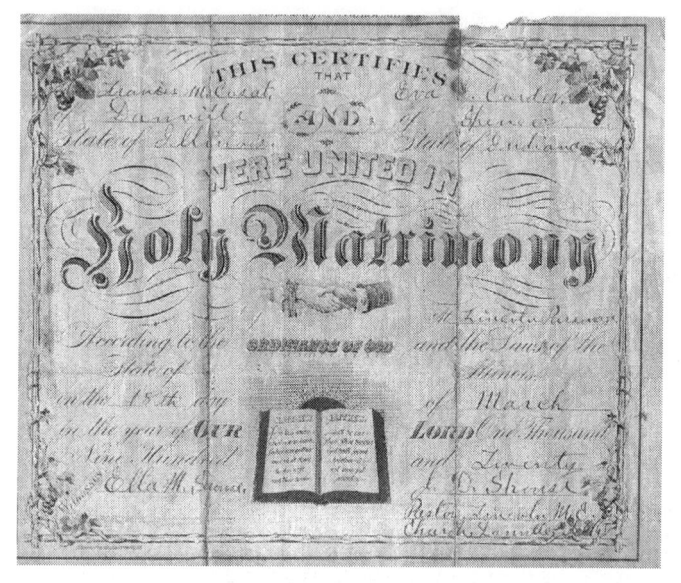

My grandpa and grandma's marriage certificate states, "This certifies that Francis M Cosat of Danville, Illinois and Eva E Corder of Spencer, Indiana were united in Holy Matrimony at Lincoln Parsonage, According to the Ordinance of God and the Laws of the State of Illinois on the 18th day of March in the year of Our Lord One Thousand Nine Hundred and Twenty."
Witnessess: Ella M Strouse and J.D. Strouse, Pastor, Lincoln M.E. Church, Danville."

APPENDIX VII

Obituary of my Grandfather, Francis M Cosat

F. M. Cosat, Ill 7 Months, Dies in Hospital

Francis Marion Cosat, 60, 206 S. Virginia Ave., life resident of Danville and retired printer employed lately by the Scott Sales Company, 814 N. Vermilion, died at Lake View Hospital at 12:50 a. m. Monday following an illness of seven months.

Mr. Cosat was injured seriously last Christmas Eve at the home of his employer, Bart Scott, 22 Dodge Ave., when an auto being backed out of the Scott driveway by a daughter, Patricia Scott, ran over him and caused injuries reported as "a severe concussion, internal injuries and a fractured pelvis."

An autopsy was performed by Dr. Harlan English to determine

Continued…

the exact cause of the illness leading to the death. Mr. Cosat re-entered the hospital last Saturday after being confined some three months following the accident.

Mr. Cosat was born Feb 19, 1889, in Danville the son of the Rev. John J. and Emma Cosat. The father was pastor of the Old Union Church northwest of Danville for many years prior to his retirement.

Mr. Cosat is survived by the widow, Eva, of Indianapolis and the following children: Mrs. Dorothy Wheatley, Indianapolis; Mrs. Mary Killeen, Gallion, Ohio; Mrs. Betty York, Robert, Glen and William Cosat, all of Indianapolis. He was preceded in death by the parents and two brothers.

Surviving also are three brothers, Everett, Theodore and Charles all of Danville, and a sister, Nell Cosat, also of Danville.

Funeral will be at 2 p. m. Wednesday at the Barrick & Sons Funeral Home where the body was taken. The Rev. Mitchell Seidler, pastor of the First Baptist Church, will officiate, with burial in Johnson Cemetery, north of Danville.

APPENDIX VIII

The annotated aerial photo on the preceding page shows a portion of northeast Blount Township of Vermilion County, Illinois as it exists today. Three generations of Cosats lived here. The dotted rectangles show the location of the original 80 acre homestead David Cosat purchased in 1835, as well as the farms of his Uncle Albert and his brothers, Henry, Peter and Jacob Commingore Cosat. Collectively the early Cosat farms covered 520 acres in this part of the Vermilion River drainage area. In 1849 David acquired additional acreage not shown below, bringing his total holdings to 235 acres. To this day, a considerable portion of Albert's 1829 land purchase remains "graced with fine stands of timber."

Northeast of David's acreage is the Old Union Christian Church where David's son, John James Cosat became pastor and Justice of the Peace. To the northwest of the old homestead David and wife Nancy Traux were buried in Fairchild Family Cemetery on Indian Creek Road near the west property line with Nancy's father Benjamin's acreage. My Grandpa Francis Marion Cosat, son of John James was buried in Johnson Cemetery outside the town of Johnsonville. Partly visible at far right in the photo, Lake Vermilion was made by damming of the north fork of the Vermilion River near Danville. Long before the land craze the river drew French fur trappers and Indians, who hunted, fished the waters and mined the cliffs above the river for the vermilion they used for their body paint. Today the largest body of water in east central Illinois, the 1000 acre Lake Vermilion serves as a public reservoir for the town and is a popular recreation area for water skiing, canoeing, fishing and camping.

APPENDIX VIV
PHOTOS

Top: This is the back section of Johnson Cemetery in Blount Township, Vermilion County, Illinois, where my grandfather Francis M Cosat lies at rest. Bottom: Visiting his grave in 2008 I say hello to grandpa for the first time in almost 60 years.

Top: This is the outside of the Old Union Church near Johnsonville where my Great Grandfather John James Cosat was pastor in the 1870's. Bottom: I stand at the entrance to the Fairchild Family Cemetery in the Illinois Nature Preserve, where my Great-Great-Grandfather, Illinois pioneer, David Cosat and his wife Nancy Truax are buried.

David Cosat's headstone in the Illinois Nature Preserve lies toppled. Others are crumbling and subsiding into the earth, some sliding down a ravine, as nature reclaims the cemetery. Are not the monuments to the lives of these pioneers, our ancestors, as worthy of preservation as the flora and fauna and the land itself?

Top: My son and I stand at the gate to the Low Dutch Cemetery of Conewago. Bottom: We pay respects at the grave of our Revolutionary Patriot ancestor, Francis Cossart.

SOURCE BIBLIOGRAPHY

1. Passenger List of the Purmerlander Kerk, sailing vessel of the Dutch West India Company, October 12, 1662
2. History of the Bloody Massacres of the Protestants in France in the year of our Lord, 1572, Jacques-Auguste de Thou, London, 1674
3. Memoir of Richard Henderson, principle founder and promoter of the Transylvania Land Company
4. Adventures of Daniel Boone, John Filson, 1784
5. Journal of Daniel Trabue, ca. 1820
6. War Records, History of Appomattox Campaign, Colonel Thomas S Allen, 1865
7. Article: Migration from New Jersey to the Conewago Colony, Pa., 1765-1771, A. Van Doren Honeyman
8. The History of New York, John Brodhead, 1871
9. History of Kentucky, Lewis Collins, 1874
10. Centennial History of Somerset County, Abraham Messler, 1878
11. The History of Protestantism, Rev. James Aitken Wylie, 1878
12. History of Vermilion County [Illinois], H.W. Beckwith, 1879
13. History of Harlem, James Riker, 1881
14. The Land of Rip Van Winkle, A.E.P. Searling, 1884
15. Article: Excerpts from a manuscript in the Ponna Archives, The Star and Sentinel, Gettysburg, Pa., January 8, 1884
16. The Low Dutch Colony of The Conewago, Rev. J.J. Demarest, 1884
17. History of Greene County, Wisconsin, Union Publishing, 1884
18. The History of the Huguenot Migration to America, Vol. I, Charles W Baird, 1885

19. Collections of the New York Historical Society for the Year 1885, Edward F. De Lancey, George H. Moore, William Libbey
20. Proceedings of the Old Settler's Association, Danville Press, 1886
21. Knickerbocker's History of New York, Washington Irving, 1887
22. Kentucky: A History of the State, Perrin, Battle, Kniffin, 1887, Boyle County
23. The Winning of the West, Vol II, Theodore Roosevelt, 1889
24. The Hoogland Family in America, Carpenter, 1891
25. A Frisian Family - The Banta Genalogy, Theodore M Banta, 1893
26. Article: Brave Defenders of Fort Boonesborough, William Chenault, Louisville Courier Journal, August 28, 1898
27. Study Out the Land Essays, T. K. Whipple, 1900
28. The Story of Manhattan, Charles Hemstreet, 1901
29. Boonesborough, George W. Ranck, 1901
30. Dutch and Quaker Colonies in America, John Fiske, 1902
31. The Past and Present of Vermilion County, Illinois, C.G. Pearson and S. J. Clarke, 1903
32. History and genealogies of the families of Miller, Woods, Harris, Wallace, Maupin, Oldham, Kavanaugh, and Brown, by Wm. H. Miller, 1907
33. The Story of New Netherland, William Elliot Griffis, 1909
34. The Catholic Encyclopedia, Volume XIII, Edited by Dr. Charles George Herberman, 1912
35. History of the Disciples of Christ in Illinois 1819-1914, Nathaniel S. Haynes, 1915

36. The Conewago Colony - Baptisms 1769-1793" by A. Van Doren Honeyman, Somerset County Historical Quarterly Volume 4 - 1915
37. This country of ours; the story of the United States, Henrietta Elizabeth Marshall, 1917
38. A Chronicle of the Ohio Valley and Beyond, Frederic Austin Ogg, 1919
39. Dutch and English on the Hudson, A Chronicle of Colonial New York, Maud Wilder Goodwin, 1919
40. History of Shelby County, Kentucky, George L Willis, 1929
41. The Cossart Family, Joseph A Cossairt, 1936
42. The Compendium of American Genealogy, 1937
43. The Cossart Family History, published by the Cossart Family Association, 1939
44. A Brief Historical & Genealogical Sketch Of The Name and Family Of "COSSART" or "COZART", Mary Ethel TILLEY, ca. 1943
45. The Fighting Frontiersman - The Life of Daniel Boone, John Bakeless, 1948
46. The Historical Review of Berks County, Pennsylvania, April 1949
47. History of the Crusades, Sir Steven Runciman, 1951
48. Miscellaneous Historical Articles on Adams County, Pennsylvania from The Gettysburg Times, 1940 - 1960
49. The Days of the Upright, A History of the Huguenots, O.I.A. Roche, 1965
50. Mercer County, Kentucky Marriage Records, 1786-1800, compiled by Elizabeth Prather Ellsberry, ca. 1965
51. American Descendants of Chertien DuBois of Wicres, France, Compiled by William Heidgerd for the Huguenot Historical Society, Inc., 1968, 1998
52. SHIP PASSENGER LISTS; NEW YORK AND NEW JERSEY 1600-1825; Edited and pub. by Carl Boyer III, Newhall, Ca., 1978

53. Westward into Kentucky: The Journal of Daniel Trabue, University Press of Kentucky, 1981
54. The Low Dutch Company : a history of the Holland Dutch settlements of the Kentucky frontier, Vincent Akers, 1982
55. "THE COZAD FAMILY" by Clerissa H. Tatterson; Jan-Mar, 1985, VOL. IV Hacker's Creek Journal
56. Abstract of Graves of Revolutionary Patriots, Volume 1-4, Patricia Law Hatcher, Pioneer Heritage Press, 1987
57. A Tabulated Genealogy of the Family of Jacques Cossart Jr. & Lea Villeman, Dee Ann (Shipp) Buck, 1991
58. The American Revolution in Indian Country, Colin G Calloway, 1995
59. Frontier Illinois (History of the Trans-Appalachian Frontier), James E Davis, 1998
60. Journal of the Ohio Historical Society, Volume 21, 1998
61. Conquest of a Continent, Theodore M Banta, 2000
62. The Complete Idiot's Guide to the Reformation and Protestantism, James S. Bell and Tracy M. Sumner, 2002
63. Seven Ages of Paris, Alistair Horne, 2002
64. Article: Plague on the Prairie, Illinois Heritage, Volume 5, Number 1, Jan/Feb, 2002
65. Cross of Languedoc, Journal of the National Huguenot Society, Spring, 2004 Issue
66. The Conquest Of The Old Southwest: The Romantic Story Of The Early Pioneers Into Virginia, The Carolinas, Tennessee And Kentucky 1740 To 1790, Archibald Henderson, 2004
67. Peter Stuyvesant, the Last Dutch Governor of New Amsterdam, John S. C. Abbott, 2004
68. Family Maps of Vermilion County, Illinois, Gregory A Boyd, 2007

69. The DuPont Genealogy, commissioned by the DuPont family of Delaware and housed in the South Caroliniana Library in Columbia, SC.
70. Patriot Index of the Daughters of the American Revolution
71. Kentucky Land Records, Lincoln County, Book 1
72. Madison County Deed Book I, pages 191-7
73. NY Colonial Manuscripts, Vol. 10, Part 2
74. The Archives of Pennsylvania, Third Series, Volume 21
75. U.S. Federal Census Data, 1810 - 1930
76. U.S. Military Pension Records
77. U.S. Military Draft Registration Records
78. Illinois Statewide Marriage Index
79. Illinois Public Land Purchase Database
80. Indiana Marriage Records, Marion County
81. Vermilion County, Illinois Mortality Census, 1880
82. Records of the Illinois Old Soldier's Home
83. Miscellaneous Family Photos and Documents

Made in the USA
Lexington, KY
26 May 2012